THE WORLD IN BETWEEN

THE WORLD IN BETWEEN

Christian Healing and the Struggle for Spiritual Survival

BY

E. MILINGO

former Archbishop of Lusaka, Zambia

Edited, with Introduction, Commentary and Epilogue, by
MONA MACMILLAN

C. HURST & COMPANY, LONDON
ORBIS BOOKS, MARYKNOLL, NEW YORK 10545

First published in the United Kingdom by
C. Hurst & Co. (Publishers) Ltd.,
38 King Street, London WC2E 8JT
and in the United States of America by
Orbis Books, Maryknoll, New York 10545
© C. Hurst & Co. (Publishers) Ltd., 1984
Printed in Great Britain

ISBNs
(Hurst) *Cased:* 1-85065-005-5; *Paper:* 1-85065-006-3
(Orbis) 0-88344-354-6

CONTENTS

PUBLISHER'S NOTE

With Archbishop Milingo's approval, the extracts from his writings published in this book, both long and short, have been re-edited. Most of them were printed on duplicating machines as pamphlets, open letters or speech transcripts, with little editorial preparation. In the present work, where it has seemed that meanings are not clear for the anticipated worldwide readership of the book, explanations have been added and existing passages rewritten, in full consultation with the Archbishop. Thus, any reader wishing to go back to the Archbishop's writings in the form in which they were originally issued will find that passages purporting to be the same will show differences in expression and sometimes in emphasis.

Throughout the book, two sizes of type have been used. The larger size has been used exclusively for Archbishop Milingo's own writings, and the smaller size for the contributions of Mona Macmillan.

Extracts from the following published writings of Archbishop Milingo have been used in this book:

Healing (Lusaka, 1976).

The Church of the Spirits (Lusaka, 1978).

Precautions in the Ministry of Healing (Moshi, Tanzania, 1978).

Plunging into Darkness (Luanshya, Zambia, 1978).

The Demarcations (Teresianum Press and Multimedia Centre, Lusaka, 1981).

Jubilee Celebrations of the Archdiocese of Lusaka, 1978.

Open Letter to my Brother Bishops and Members of the Zambian Episcopal Conference (Lusaka, 1981).

Black Civilisation and the Catholic Church (Abidjan, Ivory Coast, 1977).

My Call to Save the World with Jesus (Spiritual Retreat for Priests, Moshi, Tanzania, 1978).

Morality and Virtue (address to the Societies of Jurists and Spiritualists, New Delhi, India, 1979).

The Divinisation of Man (Conference on Missionary Awareness, Lusaka, 1980).

Father, Son, and Holy Spirit (Lusaka, 1981).

Liberation through Christ, (Divine Word Centre, London, Ontario, 1977).

My Prayers are Not Heard (Rome, 1982).

INTRODUCTION*

Emmanuel Milingo was for fourteen years Archbishop of Lusaka, a large archdiocese centred on the capital city of Zambia. In 1982 he was recalled by his superiors to Rome to silence controversy which had arisen over his pastoral methods. The controversy had many aspects and went back to the beginnings of his archepiscopacy, but it was brought to a head by his practice of spiritual healing. The following pages contain extracts from several booklets which Milingo has written, in which he describes how he discovered his gift of healing although he cannot explain it except as the fruit of faith and prayer.

His account is a pragmatic one, not a subjective analysis. He also gives a vivid impression of the spirit world that confronted him in the minds of his people; he responded to their extreme need, physical distress and confusion of mind. Their traditional structures were broken, but they still believed in a plethora of spirits which European missionaries refused to take seriously. The missionaries, severely rationalistic, told the people that the spirits did not exist, but to no avail; they continued to believe in them even when they had accepted Christianity. Milingo felt able to deal with their problems, through a combination of African sympathy and Christian belief. He did not ask for the gift of healing which he found himself to possess, and which puzzled and surprised him.

In these pages he champions African spirituality and demands recognition for it, but he also insists that spiritual healing and in particular the problem presented by evil spirits are not African phenomena only, but occur everywhere. In answer to those who say that he is himself attacking African tradition by exorcising the spirits, he maintains that there is a distinction between the benign influence of ancestral spirits and the evil which is common to the whole world. He has no desire to found an African church, but is a firm believer in the Church Universal, and only desires to be accepted by it; this is shown by the meekness with which he has received some very harsh treatment. He says 'I love the Church and would like to see her a steady

* I acknowledge with gratitude the help given me in the preparation of this Introduction by the following: on the life of Archbishop Milingo — Sister Pia Troendle of the Dominican Sisters, Ndola, Zambia; on the Church in Zambia — Father Hugo Hinfelaar, WF Chinsali, Zambia; and on the Church in general (including the list of ecclesiastical documents on page 138) Father Alberic Stackpoole, OSB, St Benet's Hall, Oxford. *Mona Macmillan*.

1

vessel on the sea, overcoming the winds blowing from all sides and corners' (*Liberation through Christ*, p. 16).

Milingo was born on 13 June 1930 at Mukwa village, in the diocese of Chipata in the eastern Province of Zambia. He comes from the Nguni people, of whom the Zulu are the oldest branch. In the early nineteenth century a body of the Zulu in South Africa rebelled against their militarist Chief Chaka and headed north. The main body formed the Matabele nation in southern Zimbabwe, while offshoots went further west to the region of Lake Malawi, now western Malawi and eastern Zambia. Milingo is of the Zambian Nguni. Until he was twelve years old he herded his father's cattle, as was the duty of many African boys. (One thinks of the young David out tending the flocks when the Prophet Samuel came to his home.) This pastoral occupation was not as peaceful as it sounds. The Zulu have a reputation for fighting and the Nguni boys were taught to defend themselves, and even encouraged to challenge each other in the rivalries that took place between them. True to this fighting tradition, Milingo finds it hard to accept injustice or untruth. He has at times been called harsh, and he is certainly impulsive and forceful in speech. He says of himself, 'I may express my views as if they were dogmas or ultimatums, but they are not intended to be. It is because I am presenting a viewpoint which comes from the depth of my heart, full of enthusiasms and emotions' (private letter, 1983).

Education was still scanty, and Milingo was lucky when in 1942 the White Fathers (the Society of Our Lady of Africa, instituted by the French Cardinal Lavigerie expressly as missionaries for Africa) opened a school close to his village. He had a friend whose father was a Catholic catechist (his own parents were practising Catholics), and the two boys decided to enrol in the new school without even telling their families. Because he had had no previous schooling (and had never spoken English), Milingo was put with the dull boys, but although he had a struggle to begin with, in the end he was the only one of the first twenty-seven to be promoted to the Junior Seminary. At that time his first name was Lotte, but he was so shocked by the story of Lot and his wife that he asked for it to be changed, and chose Emmanuel.

He had to go as a boarder to the Junior Seminary which was at Kasima in Malawi. It was while he was there that his mother died. He was deeply attached to her and deeply grieved that she had died while he was away from home. From then on he took comfort in a special devotion to Mary the mother of all Christians. He shows an unusual understanding of and sympathy with motherhood, speaking of priests as bearing 'spiritual children' and becoming mothers. He speaks of God as mother: 'The devil hunted the human race and separated us from our Mother God. We had never experienced a lonely life without our Mother, and like the baby animal left alone, may not survive. But that hunted mother of the baby animal traces back her baby and gives her nourishment, and protects the baby with new vigour and new tactics to escape the enemies. We too were lost and separated from our Mother. God traced us back and once more we are reunited to Him' (*My Call to Save the World with Jesus*, p. 29).

In the early days many African boys received their education in seminaries, which were the only secondary schools. Some of them went on eventually to become even Cabinet ministers, but only a few finished their training and became priests. Even Milingo once ran away, but was sent back by his shocked family. But he clearly made the Christianity he was taught his own, and his intimate knowledge of Scripture is evident in all he writes. He was ordained to the priesthood on 31 August 1958, and thereafter his career progressed rapidly. He was a curate for two years, and then went for a year's course at the Institute of Pastoral Sociology in Rome where he took a diploma. In 1962−3 he continued his studies at University College, Dublin, taking a diploma in education. He was then parish priest in the Chipata Cathedral for a year before going in 1966 to Lusaka as Secretary for Communications of the Zambia Episcopal Conference. In that capacity he attended a Radio Training Course at the All Africa Conference of Churches Training Centre in Nairobi. He became a 'radio priest', known throughout Zambia for his broadcasts and the radio discussions which he conducted. Of these he has written: 'In my experience as a broadcaster I gained more from a group of participants in a programme where I merely solicited a discussion. If I left the subject in skeleton form, without meat, and only introduced it to the participants, they clothed it themselves. Often I was amazed to find how much people knew about things, and if they had not been asked I would never have known' (from a report on communications).

During this time he formed ideas on African culture and the relation of the Church to newly independent Africa. At the same time he became involved with the poor of Lusaka, and created the Lusaka Helpers' Club which drew on well-to-do Christians of all races and denominations to help; it still runs a mobile clinic. His obvious talents brought him to the notice of the then pro-Nuncio of the Holy See who recommended him as the successor to the retiring Archbishop. He was appointed in June 1969 as the second Archbishop, and consecrated in August by Pope Paul VI on his visit to Uganda.

Lusaka was a more difficult assignment than most. As the capital city it draws numerous people from all regions of the country; they do not all speak a common language and are from different and often rival tribes. Many are unemployed and those who have employment are poorly paid and badly housed, and often suffer from malnutrition

with its numerous mental and physical effects. As a contrast, there is a
large white expatriate community with fine houses. These include
senior staff of multinational companies, embassies and United
Nations agencies, and they are matched by an African élite of cabinet
ministers, Members of Parliament, party officials, and civil servants of
all ranks. Lusaka did not grow as a capital, but was created. It had no
strong local population, and to serve this conglomerate of uprooted
people there were too few priests. Most parishes were served by the
Jesuit Mission, and to begin with Milingo had only one diocesan parish
priest within the capital. He had to call on volunteer priests from many
European countries — Poland, the Netherlands, Germany and
Ireland. Lusaka is outside the Province of the White Fathers, although
some of their members joined his Secretariat; since before it became
the capital it had been under a long-established Jesuit Mission, coming
originally under the Polish Vicariate, and this held the loyalty of the
white expatriates. The Jesuit church is in the town centre, but when
Milingo took over, the Cathedral had still to be built. It was erected on
land belonging to the Catholic Church at Roma on the outskirts of the
town, a district fast becoming a rich suburb, but also close to the
poorer African suburbs and shanty towns.

When in 1973 Milingo discovered his power of healing, he was
amazed and disturbed by the large numbers who appealed to him for
help. He felt he could not refuse them. If Morris Maddocks is right, in
The Christian Ministry of Healing, that man has not been prepared
spiritually for the great changes which have come about in his environment, and that therefore modern man needs the ministry of healing in
a very urgent way, then Lusaka was a place where one might expect
such a need. Change had overtaken the people in an especially cata-
strophic way. It had resulted in the disruption of community, and the
disappearance of the functions and roles that linked the individual to
it. This was particularly so for the women who had lost much of their
old dignity and status and were often left alone to support their
children, and bear the brunt of urban struggle and poverty. Large
numbers of women came to Milingo for healing.

Everywhere in Africa healing has been a function of religion. This
may be because disease is so prevalent, so much part of everyday life,
and people have been so powerless to deal with it. Not only are there
numerous practitioners within the African tradition of healing, but
the many independent Christian churches have made healing a
central part of their ministries. In his account of these churches (*Zulu
Zion*), Bengt Sundkler says: 'In a world of distintegration, danger and
disease, they all claim to function as a refuge of health and wholeness.
Healing is the need of their fellow-men and this they all attempt to
provide. With this they give to uprooted and lonely men and women

the warm fellowship and loving concern — not seldom by way of tactile expression — which they are seeking.' Milingo respects these breakaway churches for their use of the Bible and acknowledgement of the Holy Spirit, but they have generally depended on a single prophet figure, and the example of this charismatic type of leadership must have been in the minds of Church and state authorities in Zambia when he drew such a huge following through his healing. One such prophetess, Alice Lenshina, had already caused division in the country. Milingo always disclaimed any desire to form a breakaway movement, and his conduct has proved this; but, apart from that, orthodox Christians would be afraid of his being seen as just another *sing'anga* or traditional healer, perhaps more powerful and certainly cheaper than the rest. He himself wrote in a private letter: 'There are a thousand and one African doctors who claim to have mysterious powers. They charge a lot of money and they can't stand that I have the people they would have had.' He also told a friend that when his healing sessions ceased, he heard the drums beating again in the night for the African healers, which had been silent during his ministry.

Missionaries have always dismissed the whole of African religion as animism if not witchcraft, and wished their converts to break with it entirely. This attitude grew up before the researches of Freud and Jung into human psychology, and before a body of anthropological research into African customs had been accumulated. Much research remains to be done, and will be done one day by Africans themselves. In recent years the pronouncements of the Catholic Church have tended towards a less rigid view of indigenous religious beliefs, and have recommended adaptation and 'inculturation'; the blanket description of animism can be broken down into many categories of experience, spiritual or physical. Witchcraft — in the sense of using the occult for the purpose of bringing some evil to an individual, generally for revenge — is seen as no integral part of African religion. In the above sense it is proscribed by law in Zambia, and it has offended and shocked Zambians when Milingo has been accused of practising it. In spite of the official pronouncements of the Church, Milingo can still quote missionaries who say that they came to Africa to teach Africans sense. In fairness to them, they see the rule of spirits over the daily lives of their people, and especially the fear of witchcraft, as weakening and inhibiting, and they believe that they brought the freedom of Christ from all this. Their trouble is that they have not known how to deal with it, and Milingo believes that he is able to do so. He also believes that he brings freedom. He says: 'Whether we call their sufferings the "mashawe" phenomenon, they all have a right to the liberating power of Jesus Christ. . . . This thing called an "African phenomenon" has made many people seek help from the Church.

Those who have been able to be served and healed have come to know that God cares for them. They have realised that God is powerful above all other gods. They give up their beliefs in the agents of the evil one, with their multiple demands from their clients. They are redeemed and liberated from the tyranny of demonic oppression' (*Open letter to the Zambian Episcopal Conference*, pp. 12–13).

The manifestation of African religion which most puzzles and alienates Europeans is spirit possession, and it was Milingo's frequent exorcisms of those believed to be possessed which offended many of the white priests in Zambia. They thought it cheapened a power of the Church which should only be used sparingly, and encouraged the people to accept as reality something that was only in their imaginations. Milingo does indeed appear to accept the spirits as reality, but he also says that it is his duty to enter into the minds of his people, to whom the spirits are real, and that he has to speak to 'first-century Christians'. The anthropologist Godfrey Lienhardt writes of the Dinka that 'even a small boy can give a convincing imitation of possession', and that 'in some situations possession is expected and even desired; at sacrifices men, and women also, become temporarily possessed, and nobody pays much attention' (G. Lienhardt, *Divinity and Experience*, Oxford, 1961, p. 64). This desired possession is looked on as closeness to God, and often as a way of receiving messages from what Milingo calls 'the world in between'. This is not the possession that requires exorcism. William van Bensinbergen, in *Religious Change in Zambia*, distinguishes between momentary possession and chronic or permanent possession, and I.M. Lewis talks of 'mainstream' and 'peripheral' possession, the latter being a 'cult of protest' (I.M. Lewis, *Ecstatic Religion*, Penguin Books, 1971, p. 35). 'In peripheral cults the circumstances which encourage the ecstatic response are precisely those where men feel themselves constantly threatened by exacting pressures which they do not know how to combat or control, except through those heroic flights of ecstasy by which they seek to demonstrate that they are the equals of the Gods. Thus if enthusiasm is a retort to oppression and repression, what it seeks to proclaim is man's triumphant mastery of an intolerable environment. Possession is ritualised rebellion' (Lewis, op. cit., p. 111). Van Bensinbergen sees in individual manifestations of the cult of affliction egotistical attempts to force attention and money gifts from relatives.

The 'cult of affliction', then, would seem to be applicable to mashawe, a form of spirit possession widespread in Zambia but little understood, most common among women, and one of the diseases Milingo was successful in treating. Of it he says:

Here we enter into an ancestral spirits' world which so poorly, by many explorers, is expressed in a word *'mashabe'*. This word is not even of Zambian origin, and was brought to our country by travellers from the south who were using a slang called *cilapalapa* which includes a lot of Shona words. The word in the singular, *shabe*, means an evil spirit, if the English word 'spirit', with its hellenistic restrictions, can give a proper rendering of what Shona tribes understand. I would not like to make this a semantic dispute, but rather opt for using our own forms like *mushimu ingulu* (or *impiashi*) or *mzimu*. It would bring us to the depth of Bantu philosophy if we sincerely wanted to create a definition of what these terms mean in today's Zambia. And I strongly believe that we should rather see in this phenomenon a deep pastoral and missionary problem, than our self-satisfying search for a definition.

(*Open Letter to the Zambian Episcopal Conference*, p. 15)

The pioneer missionaries Smith and Dale, in their classic book on a Zambian culture *The Ila Speaking Peoples of Northern Rhodesia*, do not use the word 'mashawe', and do not recognise a generalised cult of possession, although they do describe specific cults. Mashawe causes derangement and fits of animal-like behaviour. Sociological and medical investigations into it are currently in progress. Milingo himself approached the consultant to the mental hospital in Lusaka to find out what was known about the disease, and was told that the sufferers could not be said to have any known mental illness. Yet because of mashawe, families have been disrupted and husbands have left their wives. It is treated by professional groups of drummers and dancers who have to be paid (it is the financial strain on families which causes van Bensinbergen to call the cult egotistical). But Milingo says that the term 'mashawe' is used by outsiders to cover a wide variety of behaviour, and that it is important to distinguish truly evil spirits from the rest. As I.M. Lewis says, 'Possession is as possession does', and Lienhardt says of the Dinka: 'Unlike us they do not think that this voluntary co-operation of the conscious person in any way invalidates his final state of possession as coming from a source other than himself. They are interested in 'what came about' rather than 'how it came about' (Lienhardt, *op. cit*).

There is in the following pages a great deal about evil spirits and the devil, and it is not easy to see where Milingo draws the line; he finds in Scripture plenty of support for the existence of evil spirits, which he also finds even in the context of the African religion he is defending. In *Black Civilisation and the Catholic Church* (1977), he writes of the 'roaming spirits': 'These can generally be the devils, the spirits of the bad angels; they may also be the spirits of the ancestors who have been angered or seek revenge.' This paper was written for the priests of Zambia, to try to convince them that they should look with more care and respect at the people's traditional beliefs, which he thought the missionaries in particular had not taken sufficient trouble to understand.

His differences with the Zambian clergy began from that point. He made remarks which hurt their feelings, such as that Africans could do without them. When he took over the archdiocese in 1969, he was critical of the state of things he found there, and expressed that criticism in retrospect in 1981 in *An Open Letter to the Zambian Episcopal Conference*:

I inherited the archdiocese of Lusaka in which the clergy were highly divided on a national basis, and the Church very vaguely established. On top of that there was little achievement in promoting local vocations. The missionary method developed was ineffective and certainly not in conformity with the missionary pronouncements of the Church. . . . My mission was that of presenting the Christian doctrine 'in a manner corresponding to the difficulties and problems by which the people are most vexatiously burdened and troubled' (*Christus Dominus*, No. 13). . . . In this field there was a lot to do in the archdiocese of Lusaka. The old traditional religion had such an impact on our people that those who had been baptised could hardly with pride carry the precious name of Christians. Their belief in an ancestral world constantly caused a departure from the Church in time of personal difficulty. . . . Most of our baptised Christians had two religions.

He says that he had to begin reform with the missionaries, and in an attempt to do this he instituted a school of languages and pastoral studies. These activities created a misunderstanding between himself and the Apostolic Nuncio. Looking back he wrote: 'It is unfortunate that this new approach, and yet an old one in other parts of the world, caused and still is causing a regrettable opposition from the representatives of the Holy See' (*Open Letter*, pp. 3–4).

Milingo saw that the common people were not being evangelised, and that the Church in Lusaka was the preserve of an élite which it had created itself, and of which it was the prisoner. These were mainly people who had received education from Catholic schools, which had enabled them to find prestigious employment. They were drawn to the Jesuit church of St Ignatius, and knew little of the parishes in which they might happen to live, or the needs of the poor. With them went the European and Asian Catholics, most of whom were wedded to the older practices of the Church. Traditionalism had the effect of reinforcing the élite and divorcing them from the ordinary population, much of it poor and deprived. As Milingo says, 'the missionaries, the old Catholics and the élite were separated from the simple people, and conflict had to come' (private letter). Milingo is not anti-white, and he valued the work the missionaries had done in the past. Preaching at the Jubilee celebrations of the archdiocese of Lusaka in 1978, he said: 'The first missionaries translated their prayer-life into their day-to-day activities. They taught religion, and people saw it lived as they watched them and prayed with them. This is how they succeeded in forming their own imitators, who cannot forget them as long as they live.'

But on this same occasion of the Jubilee he chose to call to account the selfish Zambian upper classes, in so far as they were Catholic:

The flattery that goes on in the Church in relation to those who hold high offices in Government or business has to disappear. These important people are not often told the truth because they are feared. In many instances they are spiritually the poorest. They are ignorant of even a parish programme, since the priests go to them and talk to them about their own affairs, in an effort to prove to them that priests also have practical knowledge. . . . They are so high that they cannot reduce themselves to the grass-roots level of the parish, nor can they take part in a programme which will put aside their status in life. Some of the priests have unfortunately contributed to the general ignorance of the Christians in the high social strata of life, because they teach them nothing except what they want to hear. What has happened is that the so-called tattered man and woman in the street, who are active members in a parish, know more about God than most of the academically qualified men and women. These have kept what they learnt at school, and what they perhaps hear on Sunday from a preacher, which they do not often question, but as soon as they come out of church they think of their jobs and positions only. Surely they enjoy being considered Christians, but as a matter of fact they are not.

(Jubilee celebrations, archdiocese of Lusaka, 16 July 1978)

The picture of class distinctions in Lusaka painted by Milingo was not exaggerated, but it was not likely to win him friends in high places. He had offended both the missionaries and the élite, and it was only the climax when the discovery of his healing powers brought crowds of the 'tattered men and women' to his services. To the upper classes he appeared to be bringing back a barbarism from which they had laboriously extricated themselves, and to them the crowds looked dangerous and disorderly.

As he relates in the opening section of this book, Milingo discovered his power of healing in April 1973, and in October of that year he went for a two months' Christian Renewal course at Rocca di Papa in Rome, where he says he tried to understand what had happened to him. He returned encouraged and began healing on a wider scale. The way this was received, he says, 'was as if it were the one thing the people had been waiting for.' However, this period did not last long, for it was less than a year later, in February 1974, that he received a message from the Secretariat for the Propagation of the Faith in Rome (Propaganda Fide), asking him to stop his healing ministry. A report had been sent through the Papal representative in Lusaka, whose relations with Milingo had not been good, although the conflict had begun with the previous pro-Nuncio.

It was in 1974, Milingo says, that he 'put before the missionaries how to deal with people who have such severe problems that, as they believe, only the ancestral worship may solve them. I was laughed at and condemned for involving myself in problems which are too "pagan" to be dealt with in the Catholic Church. I thought that our prayer was more powerful than the prayer of the traditional religion, and indeed I still believe so' (*Open Letter*, p. 4). Simultaneously with this exchange of views, his healing was banned. The Bishops now say that he was never 'ordered' to give up healing, but only 'asked'. For his part he did all he could to obey, 'but the people followed me wherever I was, at the office, at my home, and during my Confirmation tours.' In 1977 the Episcopal Conference conceded that healing sessions should be allowed to take place once a month, but at the end of 1977 this was withdrawn, and Milingo held his last session in February 1978 — outside the Cathedral because there were 4,000 people present. After this he was forced to leave his house to avoid the people, and he writes in his *Open Letter*: 'The distance which had been created between the Bishops and myself is a greater scandal to the ordinary Christians than what is spoken about.' A friend who was working with him at the time of the second ban says that he was most deeply hurt that the Bishops never discussed the matter with him or answered when he sent them his articles on healing. This rejection by the Church — which, as he says, had been his family since the age of twelve — caused a bitter wound.

Feeling thus totally isolated from those who should have been his friends, Milingo was greatly heartened when the Community of Charismatic Renewal of Ann Arbor, Michigan, USA, invited him in 1976 to visit them. He writes: 'It was my third year of being alone. Someone had heard of me and so for the first time I got the opportunity of being in contact with the Charismatic movement in the world.' This was a turning point; he had been feeling his way, following his intuition but not completely sure — 'never', he says, 'getting a word of encouragement from the Zambian Episcopal Conference, only a continuous fight' (private letter). Now with the Charismatics he found himself once again in a mainstream, his methods and insights shared by non-Africans, his synthesis of African thought with orthodox Catholic beliefs fully accepted. He has always been in doctrine an orthodox Catholic; his only deviation has been to syncretise some African beliefs with world Christianity. Since the first Ann Arbor experience he has drawn on the international Charismatic Renewal movement more than on any African source. He has developed with the movement. In 1976 he again attended a leadership course, and afterwards the Charismatic Convention in Virginia, USA, with 28,000 people. He did the same again in 1978 and rejoined the same group in 1979 at Lourdes and in 1981 in Rome for the commemoration of the 1000th anniversary of the declaration on the Holy Spirit in the Creed. He established a Charismatic group in Lusaka, called the Divine Providence Community (Divine Providence is the dedication of the Cathedral), which still continues, and in his *Open Letter* he declared: 'In spiritual renewal of the archdiocese of Lusaka we shall follow the forms adopted from Charismatic Renewal, because I see them as most proper to our people. I am communicating this to you so that in future no surprise will be expressed on the part of the Zambian Episcopal Conference' (p. 21).

Attempts have been made to detach Milingo from this world Charismatic movement but without success. At his interrogation in Rome, Cardinal Rossi told him that Cardinal Suenens, accepted as a leader of Catholic Charismatics, did not accept the Lusaka movement as genuine. Defending himself, Milingo answered: 'If it is not genuine it has not been intended to be so, because we have tried our best to be in contact with the genuine Catholic Charismatic movements in the world. In 1977 we received in Lusaka Ralph Martin, who is well known as a Catholic Charismatic leader and internationally accepted as such. In 1977 we sent representatives to the first East African Charismatic Conference in Nairobi; in 1978 representatives went to Dublin for the International Charismatic Convention' (Milingo's notes). In 1983 they went again to Nairobi. Since he has been in Rome, Milingo has been virtually adopted by Italian Charismatics; their friendship sustained him when he was deserted by everyone else, and they refused to be put off but demanded a hearing on his behalf at one curial office after another.

The gulf in communication and understanding between Black and White remains, and needs an African of Milingo's religious perception to bridge it. He believes that originally his healing and the possession from which he delivered people were rejected as 'only something African', although he pointed to them in Scripture and elsewhere in the religious world. The dismissal of everything African as of no account reflects a limited and limiting view of African humanity. Milingo says again:

Many missionaries on the one hand describe everything African as superstition or psychic deformation, and on the other hand represent the very 'one-sided rationality' so strongly rejected by the late Pontiff [Paul VI]. No wonder that I feel my vocation is to become a missionary to missionaries. . . . It may be true that I have been in a hurry to take the words of Pope Paul VI literally. Why not? There will be no exaggeration if I do so since he ordained me Archbishop of Lusaka in 1969. . . . He said words about Africa which still ring in my ears after many years: 'We think it opportune to dwell on some general concepts, charac-teristic of the ancient cultures of Africa, as their moral and religious value demands. . . . As a firm foundation there is in all traditions of Africa a sense of the spiritual realities. This sense must not be understood merely as what scholars of the history of religion at the end of the last century used to call animism. It is something different, something deeper, vaster and more uni-versal. It is the realisation that all created realities, and in par-ticular visible nature itself, are united with the world of invisible and spiritual realities. As for man, he is not considered as mere matter or limited to this earthly life, but is recognised as having a spiritual active element, so that his mortal life is seen as con-nected at every moment with life after death' (*Africae Terrarum*, 1967 — to the Hierachy and Peoples of Africa).

The Pope put it well and clearly. We have traditions and cul-tures worth consideration. But how is it that we have still to struggle so much in order to present the needs of the Africans in the Church? The comments of other Vatican documents confirm what the Pope said as an accepted doctrine in the Church. We read: 'The Catholic Church holds in great regard the moral and religious values proper to the African traditions, not only because of their own significance but because she sees them as a providential and most fruitful foundation on which the Gospel can be based and a new society centred on Christ can be built. . . . In fact the doctrine and redemption of Christ fulfills, renews and perfects whatever good is found in all human traditions. Therefore the African who is consecrated as a Christian is not forced to renounce his own self, but assumes the ancient values of his people "in spirit and in truth" ' (*Acta Apostolici Sedis*, 59, 1967, pp. 1077−8,1080). How nice it is to read all this. I am waiting for the day when it will be a reality. It will never be a reality as long as Western Christianity divides the Gospel into a way of life and a law. . . . One wonders sometimes as one observes that in some instances the preacher and teacher show no feeling for the disciple whom they teach. They are teachers and feel that they have nothing to learn from the disciple. The question is that of the Gospel: 'What good can come out of Nazareth?' Put it in your own words, and insert 'Africa' where you know it should be inserted.

(*Demarcations*, pp. 118−19)

The experience of Archbishop Milingo (see in more detail in the Epilogue) is of great importance not only for the archdiocese of Lusaka, or even for the Charismatic movement, but for the whole Church. It should be studied as a sociological model of the present situation of the developing Church. It encapsulates the complexity of old and new, and shows up the weak points — the gap between the theory expressed in ecclesiastical documents and their putting into practice, the relaxation of authoritarianism and paternalism taking place too slowly, the lack of a common spiritual language, and the consequent lack of mutual comprehension. Perhaps it can be summed up as a lack of willingness to listen to each other. Milingo's most frequent complaint against Westerners is that they will not find the time or the patience to listen. Africa needs a voice that will be listened to, and he at least has had the courage to make his voice heard. What he says is in accord with his brother African Bishops at their Synod in Rome in 1974, and they in turn were following the Declaration of Vatican II on Missions, which says: 'The Church must insert herself into the communities of people as part of the same drive by which Christ himself, through his incarnation, allowed himself to be bound by the social and cultural conditions of the people with whom he lived' (*Ad Gentes*, p. 10).

1

DISCOVERY OF THE GIFT OF HEALING

[Milingo's pamphlet *Healing* was written in 1976. In it he describes the discovery of his gift and the treatment he received because of it from his colleagues and superiors. Although that was eight years ago, the persecution has continued up till the time of this book going to press.]

I want to tell of the gift the Lord gave me in order to heal the sick. First I say in humility and gratitude,
'Everything comes from you, Lord.
You are our Creator. You gave us life.
You also keep us alive.
We thank you for what has taken place among us
in the healing of our sick brethren:
men, women and children.'

The origins of my gift of healing

There was a woman who had suffered for five months. She sometimes spent months on end without eating anything: she could only take water or soft drinks. She feared her child because she did not think him a human being. She constantly heard voices speaking to her. She was treated at a mental hospital, but to no avail.

On 2 April 1973 she came to my office and explained her problem. I told her that we should pray together. She came back a few days later and once again told me her full story. I brought her to my residence where I heard her Confession, then we celebrated Mass. But in spite of all this the voices continued and she still feared her own child. At that time I did not know how Satan behaves when he is in possession of someone. I contemplated various ways of helping the woman when suddenly an idea glowed in my mind: 'Look three times intently into her eyes and ask her to look three times intently into yours. Tell her to close her eyes the third time and order her to sleep. Then speak to her soul after signing her with the sign of the Cross.'

I carried out this instruction systematically. The woman was overshadowed by the power of the Lord, and she relaxed and became calm so that I was able to reach her soul. I prayed as much as I could, then woke her up. Neither of us knew what had happened to us. I can only explain my part of the experience. After praying for the woman my body remained so cold that I was unable to do any further work. This was because I had experienced prayer both in body and soul — with my *whole* self. I wondered how I was going to be released from this power. But gradually, by the power of the Lord, I regained my consciousness and self-mastery.

We can thank the Lord that this woman has remained well to this day. Although she has problems, they are of a different nature, she eats well, she hears no voices and does not fear her child.

I can remember a great deal that happened in the month of May 1973. I knew that the Lord was leading me to the healing of the disease of which many of my fellow-Zambians are victims — mashawe. This disease cannot be treated in a hospital. During the whole of May I thought out the different ways by which I could help my sick brothers and sisters.

I attended the Catholic Action meeting at Roma Cathedral on 3 July 1973, but was hesitant as to whether I should speak of this to the whole group. But on this occasion the Lord gave me the courage to say to them, 'Brethren, we have for a very long time suffered from mashawe, and we have had to find the doctors outside our own Church. We can heal this disease in our own Catholic Church. So if any of you suffer from this disease, let them come forward and we shall try to help them.' This was how I started publicly healing the sick in July 1973.

Two days later I started using my hand to communicate the healing powers. I went at night to the house of a man who had been poisoned. There was very little light in the room and it was quite inadequate. Thus I could not look at the man so as to communicate with him. But fortunately and by the guidance of the Lord Jesus I found another way. With my right hand I held the man's right hand and told him to relax, which he did. I poured cod liver oil into hot water, blessed it and gave it to him to drink. This made him sweat profusely. Then we took him out of the house into the fresh air for some time. He survived till 1976, when the Lord called him to Himself. He died of a different disease.

I was in Kabwe on 8 July 1973, and was healing the sick after Mass. I used my right hand to communicate what people call healing radiations. Those who had mashawe began to shout and cry. We prayed for them. One of them had been carried to the church on a bicycle but she walked home after the healing. I began to believe that the Lord Jesus approved of what I was doing. But I still did not understand the source of this power. On 24 July I was again in Kabwe and a lot of sick people came. There were so many that holding each one of them by the hand was an impossible task. The Lord Jesus showed me another way. I stood in front of the sick, and ordered them to relax and close their eyes. Surprisingly they all slept except one women who slept only after I had touched her hand.

'*Malodza a kwa Mulungu*', 'This is something like a mystery from God.' I find no better way than what I have roughly translated here to describe what befell me. It is indeed appropriate to say 'what befell me'. I did not know what was taking place in my body. I remember that one day in April 1974 I was in my sister's house at Kitwe. As I explained to her what had befallen me, she just exclaimed, 'There goes the son of my mother, nobody knows what he has.' It was difficult to explain to other people. For this reason I appeared on some days like a madman who constantly uttered things in what seemed to others a new and incomprehensible way of speaking — with nothing explained.

On 6 July 1975, I visited Luanga church and one priest helped me in healing the sick. He was surprised to notice that when the healing powers of the Lord became activated even the young infants fell asleep. Later he said, 'Strange, it is not easy to explain what it is that makes even the infants sleep.' These are in brief the strange doings of God since we do call upon His name as the people get healed. But the Lord our God does not reveal to us exactly how he performs the healing. I ended by reciting, extempore, the following prayer:

'Not even one of us was present, Lord, when you created man. Praise be to you, Lord.

We are grateful to you since we are the recipients of your
  blessings.
Praise be to you, Lord, praise be to you always.
Glory is yours in heaven and on earth.'

Trouble with headquarters

'A good thing is born with troubles.' Our own mothers have
problems in bringing forth and rearing children. Our life comes
into the world through a terrible pain. Our mothers are often
uncertain as to whether they will be able to cross the river of
darkness, and bring us to the other side, the side full of life and
light. But since they love us they close their eyes to the pain, and
to the faults of their children and open their eyes only to the
good. But this in no way means that the problems are lessened;
they are merely accepted.

I cannot tell you that I had such a faith, as this would be a lie. I
did not willingly accept the problems when they came, for the
simple reason that I myself did not recognise the gift God was
giving me, nor did I ask for it. But in His will, kindness and
ownership over me, He did surprise me by offering me such a
gift. What also surprised me was the fact that some people had
already understood and had explained to Rome what was at
stake. And Rome sent a letter blaming me and ordering me to
stop. As I read the letter I was astonished by two things, first that
while I was still trying to understand what had befallen me, some
people had already written to Rome and declared that what I
was doing was evil, and secondly that the headquarters in Rome
did not take the trouble to send someone to come and see for
himself what was happening. These were difficult days for me.
For several months I became like a fugitive in trying not to dis-
obey the order. I ran away from the sick people. I used to come
home on Thursdays at times as late as 10 o'clock at night. My
heart was attracted towards the sick. But I had to obey.
Although for several months I avoided them, the sick continued
to come.

[Francis MacNutt in his book *The Power to Heal* describes the impor-
tunities of the sick and the difficulty of obtaining any rest from them.
He points to Jesus sometimes trying to protect himself from the
crowds.]

I tried to find some consolation. I was eager to know the feelings of the Zambian clergy on the matter, and had a meeting with them on 4 February 1974. Some complained that they were tired of continually defending me since the number of people coming for the Thursday healing was constantly increasing. Others complained that they found no privacy in the house as it was all filled up with the sick. Still others stated that some nuns made a mockery of the whole thing. They said that one nun during a healing session pretended to be sleeping when in actual fact she was not. May God forgive her soul. It was impossible for them to take a common stand, and so they sent my two Vicars-General to the pro-Nuncio. I do not remember that I ever experienced anything more hurtful and shocking than this.

A further meeting with the priests of the archdiocese and others interested took place on 8 February to explain to them the nature of the healing mission. I had a strange dream the day before the meeting. The Lord Jesus said to me, 'If they do not believe that the powers you have are God-given, you should take an egg and hold it for a time in your right hand till it warms up. You then break it open and out of it will come a chicken.' The lesson I learnt from this dream was that in order to convince the people I should do things contrary to the expectations of the laws of nature. On the very day of the meeting, a woman suffering for ten years from mashawe came to see me. I explained to her that I was not allowed to use my healing powers, but even so she refused to go. She explained that no husband wanted to stay with her and she had already lost three husbands, all of whom had left her because of the disease. And she had not been able to find help from anywhere.

Up till then I had not grasped the meaning of the dream, but then suddenly I did. The Lord brought the sick woman while the case-hearings were on. Without much reflection I brought the woman with me to the meeting, and after I had spoken to the priests for some time I called her and healed her in the sight of all. Some were astonished and wondered. Others jeered and mocked. Not one diocesan priest stood up to defend me. I left the place completely disappointed and demoralised. At the meeting I had felt as if I were being called upon to defend myself for a wrong I myself knew nothing of. I did not know what crime I had committed, or who it was that I had wronged. I did not know what I was being forbidden to do. Thus I was in no position to defend myself.

Finding no one to assist me, I went to see my sister in Mtendere. She and another lady listened to my case. They told me, 'Envy and jealousy are still common among people, even among priests. Accept those problems as God's will. Make the Lord's crown of thorns your pillow. This is part and parcel of your apostolate.' This advice gave me a boost. I had not expected to hear such words from an ordinary Christian. But I realised all the same that I was beating my head against a wall.

What pained me most was the revelation of what some priests can do when they see their own bishop in trouble. I believed then that love is a gift from God, but one which most of us don't have. We are united only as the bamboos which are knit together to make a grain-store, but which don't know one another. My sister did not want me to leave the priesthood merely because I was not able to bear my problems. I was ashamed to realise that up to 1974 I had not known the extent of the problems which I had to bear.

I do not remember who it was that advised me to write a letter to the Pope (Paul VI) without going through the pro-Nuncio or any other middle-man in Rome. I sent it on 7 July 1974. After a short time I received an answer to my letter from the Pope telling me that he had now received both sides of the story. Some time later I went to see my superiors and they advised me to stop everything gradually and without causing trouble among the people.

On 7 August 1974 I had a meeting with my consultors, which was a most frightening experience. I was accused before the Papal pro-Nuncio of using hypnotism as the healing technique. Paul's advice to the effect that 'even good and profitable gifts need not be utilised always and indiscriminately' was quoted. Some said that my shaking hands with a woman could be mis-interpreted by the people. My own consultors were divided over the issue, and this prejudiced the pronouncement of the pro-Nuncio against me. I was refused an occasion to defend myself and it was stated that the powers which I had were natural and nothing more. The letter from the Vatican stated clearly that what I was doing did not befit a man of my standing as head of the archdiocese of Lusaka.

I was completely isolated and branded as disobedient. One of the priests in his kindness told me the secret of his heart: 'Look, Your Grace, I do not want to see you being removed from the archbishopric.' Rumours were circulating that a group of my own priests had already selected a successor for me.

As early as 1974, when I had received a letter from Rome condemning me, my refuge was the Head of State, President Kaunda. He called me to see him at Mfuwe Summer Lodge in the Game Reserve, ordering that I should travel on a Zambian Air Force plane together with Mamma Kaunda, which I did. What a day it was. The condition I was in is hard to describe, but in my language I would say *'Ndinasongoka mutu'*, which means that I felt so ashamed before my Church that I had nowhere to hide my head. I remember a Zambian priest saying in February 1974, 'It is up to us to accept what the Archbishop is doing, or simply to take what Rome has said.' Then came an official pronouncement from two priests, an Indian and a Pole, *'Roma locuta, causa finita'* ('When Rome has spoken the case is finished'). A Catholic doctor came to my house to see me at work. I thought I was doing the right thing but of course it was too simple for him. He never returned, and I heard afterwards that he was the one who really pushed things in the direction they took, ascribing what had happened to auto-suggestion, hypnotism, a natural gift, and so on. The position which the Catholic doctor held would have embarrassed me later, if the President had not come in. Fortunately I reported to the President in time. At Mfuwe, I told him sincerely that there had been no preparation on my part for the reception of these gifts. It was a surprise even to me. I was not able to explain in clear terms what happens to me when I stand before the sick, but the President simply said, 'It is the result of belief. For me', he went on, 'I find no difficulty in accepting what the Lord has given you. And I would advise you not to be tempted to specialise. Leave it to God, He will show you how to use this gift.' As for my relations with the medical doctors, he said, 'You don't at all interfere with the doctors. You don't use medicine, nor do you charge the patients. And I strongly advise you not to receive remuneration.' He then told me that he was contemplating writing a book on Faith, and that what had happened to me encouraged him all the more to go ahead. Again in 1977, it was the President who on many occasions refuted the arguments of some Catholics who had planned to use all possible devices to bring my name and my person into disrepute.

How can one escape suffering? I have tried to escape it, but I failed to run away from it fast enough, with the result that it has always caught up with me and I have been vanquished. I have suffered the more because I did not accept the suffering as it came, but resisted. In the end I had to say, 'It is normal for a Christian to accept suffering since he is a follower of Jesus Christ.' The normal conclusion in this situation was, 'What else can a Christian do, but carry his daily cross?'

The prophet Jonah was ordered by the Lord to go and preach to the city of Nineveh. The message he was ordered to deliver would not be pleasing to his hearers, and so Jonah refused to be an instrument of God to bring a message of doom, sorrow and depression to the people of Nineveh. He fled by boarding a ship, going away from Jerusalem as well as from Nineveh. He forgot only one simple thing, namely that the Lord is the 'Master of water, winds and the crew of the ship'. He put his companions on board into trouble, for the Lord took revenge by almost wrecking the ship and its company — until they cast a lot which fell on Jonah as the culprit, and so he was thrown into the sea. Only then were the people on board able to sail on safely.

We read in the book of Jonah, 'Now the word of the Lord came to Jonah, son of Amittai, saying, "Arise, go to Nineveh, that great city, and cry against it, for their wickedness has come up before me! But Jonah rose to flee to Tarshish from the presence of the Lord." ' Comparing myself with Jonah, I think that I accepted the order of the Lord, but not all that accompanied its execution. To me the Lord said, 'Go and preach the Gospel.' The power of the voice left me no choice, nor did I have the courage to ask how this Gospel had to be preached. I went into myself and simply waited for a further clarification. Since that time (October 1973) the Lord has spoken to me through signs. Fortunately I was not told, like Jonah, to preach the Gospel to a specific community. But this was how I imprudently plunged myself into difficulties. The prophet Jonah was even told what to preach about. For me it was only an order 'to preach the Gospel'.

In 1976, when I was in Ann Arbor, Michigan, with the Word of God Ecumenical Charismatic Community, God spoke through the community's prophet. His message was, 'You will still have to suffer. However, you will come out of it.' The community prophet had already heard of the ordeal of suffering which had been my lot since April 1973. He was shocked, and felt sorry for me when the Lord urged him to tell me that I had to suffer still more. Anyway, the Lord had ordered him to deliver the message to me and he did it faithfully. I for my part pondered over the message, but failed to guess the nature of the suffering in store for me. I had only the consolation that the Lord had forewarned me, which was proof to me that he loves me and will be with me. The realisation of the prophecy in June 1976 is what prompted me to write these words. The sufferings have come and in many ways I have tried to dodge them, though I have not been swallowed up by a fish. But the prayer of Jonah when he was in the belly of the fish is certainly my prayer also. 'Then Jonah prayed to the Lord his God from the belly of the fish, saying: "I called to the Lord, out of my distress, and he answered me; out of the belly of Sheol I cried, and thou didst hear my voice" ' (Jonah 2. 2−3).

In all that I have passed through, the Lord has always been with me, though from time to time I ignored his presence and looked for human consolations. But I now understand the difference between being an instrument of the Lord to be used for the service of the community, and being a sharer in His life − holiness. I have still to go a long way before both are combined in me. We read in Scripture: 'Not every one who says to me "Lord, Lord" shall enter the kingdom of heaven, but he who does the will of my Father who is in heaven. On that day many will say to me, "Lord, Lord, did we not prophesy in your name, and cast out demons in your name, and do many mighty works [miracles] in your name?" And then I will declare to them, "I never knew you; depart from me, you evildoers" ' (Matthew 7. 21−25). When these prophets, about whom Jesus is speaking here, prophesied, their prophecy came true. Those who cast out devils actually sent them away. The two gifts − of prophecy and casting out devils − are gifts for the community, being communicated through ordinary human beings. The presence of these gifts in the person does not necessarily also mean the presence of divine life in that person. Steve Clark, one of the first

Catholic members of the Charismatic Renewal in the United States, comments on this text: 'He is not saying that they did not really prophesy or cast out demons or do miracles in his name. Rather, he is saying that that is not what makes a man a genuine disciple of His (someone He "knows"). What makes a man a genuine disciple of His is doing his Father's will, holiness' (Steve B. Clark, *Spiritual Gifts*).

I have often found myself asking God whether He is aware of my sufferings. How true is it that I am doing His work? Are the people I am serving aware of my personal sacrifices in serving them? What will ever remain true to me is that God's ways are not our ways. Although I did not speak directly to the Lord to reject His will, nonetheless I have often been tempted to give up the use of the gifts the Lord has given me and cease to serve the community. This seemed to me a way to go back home and enjoy personal privacy and freedom. Then someone came to see me on 22 September 1977 and said to me, 'This is a message for you. I object to your plan to give up the healing ministry. Since you have it within you, even if you resign, you will find it difficult to bury it by someone's order.' It is true that twice I have been greatly tempted to resign as Archbishop of Lusaka due to the unexpected treatment I received from my superiors in Rome. The revelation above refers to these temptations. Though I did not prefer death to life as Jonah did, I did however give way to my deep sorrow by thinking of being completely out of sight of public ecclesiastical services. While endowed with spiritual gifts, I have still remained as human as Jonah the prophet.

(*Healing*, pp. 1–2, 7–10, 17–20, 29–30)

[It is relevant to the fact mentioned earlier that some doctors and priests mocked Milingo, saying that he used only 'natural' powers, that Francis MacNutt, who had met with the same reaction, says: 'As long as we recognise that God works in his creation, we need not be threatened by recognising that some cures at prayer meetings are caused by suggestion or other such causes' (*The Power to Heal*, p. 62).

Milingo gives his own interpretation of what constitutes spiritual healing in his book *The Demarcations*:]

When we are defining 'healing' we should not limit the word to a cure for a physical ailment and only that. Healing includes the aspects of suffering which affect even the moral and spiritual life of the sick person or the petitioner. This is the only way to bring in the word 'ministry'. If the meaning of the word 'healing' were restricted to a cure for physical ailments, it could not be appropriated by the Church. Healing of this kind has existed since before the Church of today came into existence, and the Church merely followed suit with its medical services, mission hospitals, and so on. The healing we want to deal with here is a comprehensive, all-inclusive concept. We want to define the healing whose actualisation, or effective part, goes beyond the expectation of the healer, except in the case of Jesus the king of healers. The healing we want to define is basically a supernatural work, a continuation of the liberating, saving and protecting work of Jesus Christ. . . .

What is healing then? In our context healing means taking away from a person a disturbance in life which acts as a deprivation of self-fulfilment and which is considered an unwanted parasite. In whatever way we take it, the expected result is to release someone from a stumbling block to human fulfilment. This may be taken in a physical or spiritual sense. . . . We do not deny the fact that the cause of lack of fulfilment in human life may be the person to whom it happens. . . . We have a litany of mental diseases. Those of us who have dealt with this category of disease have come to realise that words and the persuasions which come from them sometimes mean nothing, even if their sounds are heard. A mental patient is sometimes one who may help us to understand what contemplation and ectasy mean. Some of the mental patients listen to a nurse, a medical doctor, or a faith healer but they are in a world of their own. Strangely enough, one notices that from time to time they will force the listener to pay attention to them. Humanly speaking it is hard to get through to them both physically and spiritually. That is why I have said above that often the faith healer is drowned in surprises by the cures that go so far beyond expectation. The healer's words sometimes seem to mean nothing to mental patients, and some of us have no clue to the science of psychology. It is all 'plunging into darkness', and often we have experienced the dawning of light and life, to the release of the patient, and to our own joy. Praise God. . . .

How often have we been laughed at by those traditionalists who claim that we are healing 'unrealities'. I remember one priest who called our healing session in Lusaka a 'hit-parade', where unhappy and unfulfilled women went for consolation from loneliness and uprootedness. We were being forbidden to heal because most of our patients were suffering from psychosomatic diseases which, according to the reasoning of our critics, needed no healing of our category. Our critics have been the most informed persons, if one may cynically say so, especially in psychosomatic, psychic or hypnotic diseases. What they lacked was the ability to give us alternatives, since the patients were there confiding their diseases to us. For us there was no alternative but to appeal directly to the One who, regardless of the nature of a disease, cured all those who came to Him — Jesus our Lord and Saviour. 'At sunset all those who had friends suffering from diseases of one kind or another brought them to Him, and laying His hands on each He cured them' (Luke 4.40–41).   (*The Demarcations*, pp. 100–4)

A medical doctor reaches the end of the road, arriving at a cul-de-sac. A faith-healer pours out his or her soul in praying for the sick, without being certain whether the target is being hit or not. In each case the answer is Jesus: He is the Word through which the doctor, the religious minister and the patient came to be. The doctor who hands over the incurable patient to Jesus will later find a companion and a friend in Jesus. The faith-healer who is in doubt as to whether the prayers being offered may be pointing downwards instead of upwards should remember that Jesus is the intercessor to His Father for the whole human race. Like St Paul, let the faith-healer say: 'So I shall be very happy to make my weaknesses my special boast so that the power of Christ may stay over me, and that is why I am quite content with my weaknesses, and with insults, hardships, persecutions and the agonies I go through for Christ's sake. For it is when I am weak that I am strong' (II Cor. 12. 9–10). We heal by the power of Christ. Sometimes Jesus treats us as apprentices, teaching us not to appropriate the gift of healing as if it were the product of our own mind. It does not even depend on us to effect the cure. For our part, we have to realise that by special favour we have been given the gift of healing to serve our brothers and sisters in need.

So 'to heal', in our context, means to heal the whole person. Jesus, after healing someone from a physical disease, is some-

times heard to say: 'My friend, your sins are forgiven you.' Sometimes the stumbling-block to physical healing may be an attachment to vice. For instance, not granting forgiveness or refusing
to accept it has delayed some physical healings, and in some
others the healing has never even taken place. It is now a
common practice, during healing sessions, to prepare the peti-
tioners for reconciliation with God and with their friends. We
feel that the starting-point for healing the whole person is the
inner healing. There have been cases where healing did not take
place just because someone believed that God had not been fair
in dealing with him or her. There have also been cases in which
the petitioner hated God — the source of goodness. So the
prayer of the petitioner would have been as follows: 'You created
me, you also created misfortune to follow me.' Hence such peti-
tioners should first ask pardon from God so that they may be
forgiven and, in turn, forgive God. One cannot ask for a favour
from someone with whom one is in a state of enmity. Sin, therefore, is one of the stumbling-blocks to the healing of a whole
person. The consequences of sin go beyond the spiritual
wounds; they cross over to the physical life of a person. In Psalm
107 we read: 'Some were sick on account of their sins and
afflicted on account of their guilt. They had a loathing for every
food; they came close to the gates of death. Then they cried to
the Lord in their need and He rescued them from distress. He
sent forth His word to heal them and saved their life from the
grave' (vv. 18—20).   (*The Demarcations*, pp. 105—6)

[In an interview with the broadcaster David Willey after his resignation, Milingo said: 'As far as I am concerned healing is just a passing
stage. What matters is to be reconciled with God; to be at peace with
God. Once that is there, we can overcome anything' (*Africa Now*,
September 1982).
    Milingo has been accused of introducing an 'African type' of heal-
ing service, and it is therefore of interest to have the following account
of the liturgy he followed, which appears in essence to be wholly
orthodox.]

In whatever state of health we are when we come to a healing
session, we must first thank God that we are still in existence.
Whatever disease we are suffering from, it could easily turn out
to be deadly. The fact that we have survived and have even come

for healing is by God's favour. For this reason and many others, we must begin every healing session with a prayer of praise. We must publicly confess that God is THE FATHER by definition. He is the source of life, not only of human life but also of all life on earth as well as in Heaven, and wherever life is. When we are sick we tend to believe that God has neglected us. But as a matter of fact He still cares for us. He gives us friends who surround us with love and concern, who share with us the pains which come from the illness. He gives us food, water, air etc. and shows us that He is present where we are in many ways. So it is good first to forget about the illness and to praise God for the many kindnesses he lavishes on us so profusely and generously:

    You changed my mourning into dancing;

    You took off my sackcloth and clothed me with gladness,

    That my soul might sing praise to you without ceasing;

    O Lord, my God, forever will I give you thanks (Psalm 30).

The presence of the Lord

What is special at a healing session, and what has attracted many people, is the presence of God. It is special because here the sick experience Him through their physical as well as their spiritual being. We first ask God to lift them up into the atmosphere where they can meet Him. With the prayer of praise, thanksgiving and adoration, God is so pleased that He accepts our invitation when we say, 'Come, Lord and let our brothers and sisters share your presence in a special way.' Then we call upon the Father, the Son, and the Holy Spirit. The sign that they have arrived or that they are there with a presence which is communicable is the profound silence, and the relaxation and gentleness which are seen on the faces of the sick. It is an experience of God's goodness among all people. The brotherhood and sisterhood of humanity is then a realisation. The selfishness is wiped away, and everyone co-operates so well when it comes to any needed assistance to one who is very sick. There is a loving closeness between each and every one of us. Here then is proved the fact that God is love, God is unity, God is Father to all of us.

Calling the Angels and Saints

For us there is no longer just a faith-relationship between us and the Angels. We rely on them during the healing sessions. Our reasons for this are
— They have kept their original beauty before God and humanity.
— They have lived in conformity with the will of God since their creation.
— They know what best to say to God and how to put it to Him. On account of this they help us to give praise to the Lord in the best way possible.
— They are our friends and wish us well in life. So we count on them during the healing session and we rely on the power of their prayers on our behalf.

The coming of the Angels has its own signs. It seems to me that they quickly disturb the presence of the evil spirits among the patients. However, since we work as a team, we reserve the power to fight the evil spirits to a special stage during the process of healing.

The calling of the Saints is a consoling experience because one feels that they have such an understanding that there is very little need to explain to them the problems of the sick. They know what we mean when we speak of epilepsy, leukaemia, asthma, continuous headache etc. Quite a number of them have experienced these diseases. We have our own favourite Saints: Mary our Mother, St Joseph, St Andrew Bobola, Sts Peter and Paul, St John Vianney (the Curé of Ars), St Thérèse of Lisieux, St Emmanuel, and Patricia (our fellow-African from Kenya). To our own list we add all the Saints as a community. We rely on them too, since they know how to put things to the Lord in the best words. This is how our prayers are effective. We are not alone.

Calling the diseases

There are patients who are unable to express the exact nature of their disease. For instance it is not easy to put into words what causes a tumour, be it an internal one in the head or in the stomach, or one on the surface of the body. These things are mostly felt when they are already advanced. Therefore the beginnings, the roots of the disease, are not known. Usually people will say, 'I have a swelling here, which started some months back, and it gives me terrible pain.' So what we do during the calling up of the diseases is to ask the Holy Spirit, the Spirit of discernment, to let us know the different diseases. The result of our prayer is that many people once more feel the pains from the diseases, and these pains extend to many parts of their body, wherever the disease has branched.

This is the sorrowful part of the healing session. Those who are epileptic fall into convulsions. Tumours become agonisingly painful and disturb the patients, many of whom scream with the pain. Those who have incurable wounds feel the burning fire on them. The possessed cry, shake, speak strange languages and twist themselves and roll on the ground. Those who are subject to phobias, anxieties and worries sometimes just weep, their tears coming down their cheeks without control. A miserable sight, but a sign of hope. The Holy Spirit has discerned the diseases, putting them in the open for us, and urges us to pray for the sick because they are really in pain and are subject to various kinds of tortures. We thank the Lord for having sent us the Spirit of discernment, and so we go on to the next stage of the healing session.

The healing prayer

The coming of the Lord Jesus Christ. This is His time. When we say 'Through Jesus Christ, in Jesus Christ and with Jesus Christ', here now is the realisation of the powers and authority of Jesus Christ over Satan, sin and death. A great moment for the sick. This is the time of healing, and we present Jesus Christ to the sick as one who is moving among them, healing each from whatever disease is being suffered. As Jesus moves among the sick, once more the evil spirits react savagely, for example making the patients roll on the floor, screaming and crying, sometimes at the top of their voices. Slowly their self-mastery returns, and some regain consciousness before the healing prayer has come to an end.

At times we direct the prayers to the individual diseases, as we have been told by the patients. But because some of the diseases are hard to name, we just say 'Lord Jesus Christ, you know every piece of what they are made of. You know what disorder has been caused in them by the diseases. Please let everything work well once more, so that our brothers/sisters may take their place in society, enjoying the health they need as a piece of work coming from your perfect hands. Heal them from all the diseases as you know and see them.'

Then we sprinkle holy water on them, and next comes the imposition of hands and the calling of the Holy Spirit to complete the work of healing by bringing our brothers and sisters to a new life, both spiritual and physical. We ask the Holy Spirit to increase Faith, Hope and Charity.

Finally we raise the crucifix and ask the Lord Jesus Christ, the crucified, to seal his work with His precious Blood, which He shed for us: 'Let them all be marked with His Precious Blood. So we pray.'

We end with a prayer of thanksgiving to the Holy Trinity, to the Angels and to the Saints. Then we ask the Lord to protect the sick and give them special blessings.   (*Healing*, pp. 35–8)

2

THE EVIL SPIRITS AND HOW TO FIGHT THEM

[Milingo has been criticised by his brother-priests for putting too much emphasis on evil spirits and resorting too frequently to the use of exorcism, which he calls the ministry of deliverance. Because of the belief in spirit possession of many kinds (see Introduction), this ministry may be asked for more often in Africa than elsewhere. But the phenomenon is not unique to Africa, and Milingo is not unique in meeting it. Cardinal Suenens says, 'We . . . need the Holy Spirit to overcome the powers of darkness. I believe strongly in the powers of darkness' (*Your God*, p. 96). And Francis MacNutt writes, 'My experience (and study) lead me to believe that evil spirits exist, that they can cause sickness, and that they can also heal by removing the sickness they cause. In most nations and cultures . . . there are witches or spiritualists who claim to curse and to heal. . . . I see no reason to deny that there is a power in spiritualism that works. The pastoral practice of the Catholic Church has always accepted the power of spirits as a real force in human affairs, although recent times have seen the ministry of deliverance played down in the Church. . . . These powers are ultimately destructive and enslaving; it is important to recognise them rather than deny them, and to learn to apply the power of the Holy Spirit in healing, so that sick people will not be driven to seek help from an alien and dangerous source' (MacNutt, *op. cit.*, pp. 74−5). This is precisely what Milingo was saying; he wanted to offer Christian healing and deliverance to people who were already seeking it from 'alien and dangerous sources'. He writes:]

With fear I have sometimes listened to people talking playfully about Satan and his demons. I have heard that some offer themselves to Satan in order to meet with good luck in life. When I talk to the devils and their chief, Satan, they tell me, 'We have no other aim than destroying a person's life'. . . . It really scares me to see how people talk lightly and proudly about Satan and his devils. The devils have no good points and they wish nobody any good. They hate human beings because the human being has still got the freedom to decide for God on the one hand or for Satan plus his devils on the other. (*Healing*, pp. 10−11)

[In his pamphlets *The Church of the Spirits*, *Plunging into Darkness* and *Precautions in the Ministry of Deliverance*, Milingo gives some idea of the confused state of African religion, which called for his ministry of deliverance. People are ready to seek help from any source. The 'Church of the Spirits' caters for this frantic search. At the same time Milingo emphasises that exorcism is not a mere matter of repeating formulae, but calls for purity of life and a determined effort towards sanctity on the part of the exorcist.]

The Church of the Spirits is a group of people who have been given spiritual power by the devil, and whose aim is unquestionably to wage war against the holy people of God. Many of these agents of the devil are living in isolation. They do really speak to the spirits, and in their name give orders to the patients. In today's Zambia they use the Bible and may even use some prayers from established churches to suit their clients. They are leading a strange life due to their vocation.

The second question is 'Who are their members?' They are usually the patients whom they have apparently healed; the patients believe they are healed and are kept in their church by the fear that if they go back to their Christian churches they will be sick again. Among these will emerge another group of disciples who will also heal later on, who are selected from among the clients. These take a course which demands a higher fee than that which they ask for healing . . . When the patients who are subject to the control of the spirits come together for healing, they also go into a trance, and act according to the orders they are given: if they are told to dance, they dance as long as they can till they are tired. This is where a human being is humiliated, becomes cheap, eats raw meat or soil, performs all sorts of strange bodily gestures, and is not aware if he/she is naked. Especially in towns where many are ignorant of what is happening, this is taken as a drama in the streets, and anyone can come and watch without paying a fee.

(*The Church of the Spirits* p. 6)

[An American research worker, Leroy Vail of the University of Virginia, was able in 1982, by paying a fee, to collect such a group of dancers and patients together in an open space in Lusaka, with casual spectators, just as Milingo describes.]

The Church of the Spirits has been discovered as working against the Church of Christ through the patients it has treated from the Christian churches. It has ordered them never to return to their respective churches or they will die. . . . The patient is reborn in the spirit and is subject to the orders of the spirits. In the end this man or woman may be married to the spirits and may get all sexual satisfaction as if he or she were married. The spirits will make it difficult for their victim to have any normal feelings which exist between a man and a woman, and if he or she is married the marital relations diminish and in the end there is no husband or wife in the family.

(*The Church of the Spirits*, p. 4)

The performance of spirit worship should not be called 'dance'. In our ecclesiastical language it should be called the liturgical ritual of the spirits. The dancer does not enjoy the game. It is an order from the spirits, and so it must be done. When they decide that the victim should stand up and dance, even if he or she is very sick, it must be done, because the spirits have ordered it. The spirits are proud: they like to dominate human beings. . . . This is to them a call to their worship. They enjoy being admired, and hence they attract people. They promise their victims that by dancing they will be healed. But as a matter of fact they continue to be sick. Dancing means that the spirits have been accepted, because they reckon this victim as one who obeys them.

There are dances to the spirits which have been approved by the community, tribal spirit dance. They are not the same as the spirit dance I am speaking about. The ancestral spirit dances have quite a lot of fixed methods of dancing. But one who dances in a trance follows the rhythm that is given by the spirits.

(*The Church of the Spirits*, pp. 22–3)

[The above quotation shows how Milingo distinguishes between African tradition and a decadent devil worship which has arisen from the insecurity of modern life. Below he describes the kind of pressures which have led to the distortion.]

Pacts with the devil

From the outset one would like to ask: 'Why on earth make pacts with the devil?' In our language we have a proverb, '*Mkango ukasauka ukudya udzu*', that is, a lion which by nature lives on meat will eat grass when meat is not available. You can imagine how much grass a lion will have to chew in order to be satisfied. He is used to swallowing lumps of meat, and when satisfied he stays for some days without eating. Then you can understand what a humiliation it would be for him to collect grass and fill his stomach with that. 'Necessity knows no law.' Many people have covered themselves with this principle, and tell us how they came to be in situations which obliged them to live above the law.

I would like to push the expression 'Necessity knows no law' further. Those who break laws when confronted with insuperable problems which seem to remove all legal restraints are bound to accept at the same time the consequences which will follow. There is no doubt at all that a lion which by nature does not live on grass will eat some poisonous grass. Hence living on grass is dangerous to a lion, because it does not have the selective instinct for choosing proper edible grass. But it reaches a stage when it has to choose between life and death. Even so, a lion is not blameless, because it is responsible for having eaten all the animals in the area. It was greedy and did not think of tomorrow.

There is another expression — 'Necessity is the mother of invention.' Even here there are risks. For example, atomic energy was discovered in the normal conditions of life, but this discovery was used to produce the Hiroshima bomb. Another example is that of the freedom fighters who have learnt to use guns, and some of them were led on by simulated friends who had no genuine care for them, except to turn them into slaves at a later stage. However, in their situation anyone who will offer them the means to liberate themselves from oppression appears good. Here again they are faced with a choice, 'to live as free human beings with dignity, or to remain forever slaves in their own homeland'. In whatever situation people find themselves, as adults they are still the masters of their own decisions.

You are still asking: 'Why on earth make pacts with the devil?' You are aware of how important it is to have wise Ministers of Finance and of Economic Planning. These two people keep the national granaries. On our behalf they travel to different countries and accept loans on a short- or long-term basis. We usually do not know all the aspects of the conditions of accepting the loans. They may be moved from their posts tomorrow, but the signed agreements remain, and the obligation to pay back the loans remains with the whole nation. If we knew to what extent they had sometimes to undergo humiliations, we, as a nation, would not accept the loans, because we have often seen that they put us into the most difficult political relationships. We have been obliged to be friends with very dishonest people, whose 'love' for us was cold and self-interested, not as we imagined from the written agreement, which sounded fine and dignified.

It is hard for me to reveal the many reasons why people make pacts with the devil and his agents. I know many reasons which, because of the respect I have for those whom I have delivered from the devil, I am not free to mention here. However, they do not come under the category of necessity; rather they are made as the result of despair and disappointment with human life and society. However, the beginnings are rooted in their own acts of imprudence in life. It is hard to justify those who want to settle their debts and be rich overnight, and find that the only one to come quickly to their rescue is the devil. But the devil makes his own conditions. He will not just say 'Yes'; he wants to be certain that you are asking for his help with your full senses about you. Hence he has often asked his clients to sign the pact with their own blood. This means that the devil gives you what you want, while for his part he is certain that he will have *you* in exchange. This is why he asks you to sign with your blood. If the devil gives you money, what can you give him in return? He will not ask you to pay the money back; rather, the fact that you say you will abide by his orders is the promise that pleases him. He will advise you on how to lead your new life, and how to bring many more people to him. He will offer you a lot more of this world's goods and will see to it that you are protected in many ways. Whatever may be the case, you are aware of the wrong means you are using to get your money.

However, not everyone who is possessed has made a pact with the devil. But the one who signs in blood offers a pledge to the devil and is certainly guilty. Anyone who subjects himself to the devil is the slave of the devil. Many people have found themselves surrounded by many misfortunes after making the pact with the devil, more than they had before. The devil is totally evil and destructive, and it is a complete fallacy to believe that he can treat anyone with a little kindness, a little mercy, a little generosity here and there. It is not in the nature of the devil to have to do with anything with even a remnant of 'goodness'. As they leave the many possessed, they confess: 'Yes, we have really troubled this one. She is lucky that you have come to deliver her. We were going to do more to her if you had not delivered her. Look what we were planning to do. . . .' At this last sentence the devils demonstrated what diseases they were going to inflict on the victim. They said that they would make her faint as she walked on the road and in the end destroy her. So they put her out completely like one who is dead, just to make me see how powerful they are. They confessed to me that this woman had been given to them by Mrs ——, who is their agent in one of the townships of Lusaka. But since they were over-powered by the authority of Jesus Christ, they would return to the agent and kill her. I did not agree. I ordered them to go back to hell and stick to their place of punishment, because I believe that as long as that woman (their agent) lives, she also needs salvation.

The gifts from the devil — wealth and prosperity

People do not believe what one writes unless one quotes a string of books as references. On the other hand I have read of many episodes of witchcraft, and am certain that most of the writers have never met a witch. They quote so many essays from research scholars who have never actually dealt with a witch. Dealing with the devil may be the same. How often have I seen holy religious shocked almost to death as they witness the tortures the devil inflicts or a possessed person. But how many books have we all read on the same issue?   Quite a number of past writers on ancestor worship have never attended a conversation between an African clan and its living-dead. All these would dare ask me: 'On whose authority do you write about witches and spirits with certitude?' I boldly say in Latin: '*Expertus potest credere.*' Having passed through the experience I can dare to write with authority and certitude. I have talked with the witches, and I have dealt with the dead. I have gone beyond theory. I too have been forced to know this by the privilege of the Lord to prove to the people that Jesus is truly one Lord and Saviour, and that He is Lord of the dead and the living. He could speak to the dead Lazarus, and was able to bring back Moses and Elijah on Mount Tabor, but always for a purpose and an approved reason.

It is a well-known fact that none of us chooses poverty just for the sake of being poor. It is humiliating to be in debt, to go about in tatters, and to live from hand to mouth. Poverty restricts a person's attitude towards life. A poor man sees each day as a torture which he cannot escape as it is not his own choice. He is preoccupied with what to eat and what to wear, and with who will listen to him as he goes begging. He reformulates his begging tactics in order that his benefactors may be moved and look at the story with a new awareness of his problem. I am speaking of genuine poverty, not poverty of the man-made variety. There are many beggars who have been made lazy by the community which has sometimes been over-generous to them, but I mean people who have tried all possible means to uplift themselves and their families, and the more they have tried the lower they have fallen. Some of these have turned to the devil and the devil has been happy to receive them. The question is: 'Did they try God? Why were they so quick to think of the devil?'

I know a boy whose family background was not very famous. He was at school and thought that he might uplift the family by getting 99% in class. However, in order to obtain the first rank, there was need to pray to the devil to hurt the one who was usually first in that class. In prayers to the devil the name of the special devil from whom one expects favours is mentioned. As I said earlier, I am not allowed to betray the secrets of those I have delivered from the evil one. At another time this boy wanted to obtain 80% in class and he prayed as follows: 'O Lord Dragon, you know that I want to work for you, and you know that I am yours. I want to obtain in the exam 80%, I pray you.' To experience his pact with the devil, that is to say to feel the devil's presence, he was told to write a letter to Lucifer. He had to write this letter on what, in the order, was called 'virgin paper', meaning an immaculately clean sheet. He had to put down his wishes and write with his 'proper blood', and say the following

prayer: 'I hereby present to you all my friends and benefactors
and my wishes, that I may have a good answer from Lucifer, the
minister of the devils, and from the State Bam — 77.' This
letter was to be sealed and addressed to 'Bam Osley, Rue 1177
Avenue, Polyenteindia de Aire', and left somewhere in the
room. The boy was to wait for the answer at midnight, leaving
his door open. His letter ended with the words 'I am your soldier
on earth.' As a matter of fact this boy did get an answer at
midnight: the devil came and took hold of him and enrolled him
in his military group. This was the beginning of his misery.

Poor boy, he never got the marks he expected, and he became
unrecognisable from his real self, so that he quarrelled with his
parents and relatives, lost friends, and became a vagabond. He
was possessed and no employer would take him for work. Even
after I had delivered him from the devil and other spirits, he did
not feel safe. He longed to stay with me at home, but it is very
hard for me to keep anyone like him, because of the shortage of
rooms at my house. On the other hand I would have liked to
follow him up, and slowly introduce him into the world and
normal life. I took away all the pledges which bound him to the
devil. He had a set of prayers to be said each day to the devil and
his spirits. He had a ring and a handkerchief and some medicines sealed in special small envelopes. The agents of the devil
subjected him to all these conditions of discipleship. On each
day of the week he had to pray to a particular devil as follows:

Sunday	Aquiet
Monday	Lucifer
Tuesday	Nambroth
Wednesday	Astaroth
Thursday	Achan
Friday	Bechet
Saturday	Nabam

This was his prayer on Saturdays: 'I swear to you Nabam, in the
name of Satan, in the name of Beelzebub, in the name of
Astaroth, and in the name of all other evil spirits, that you come
to me; come just now to me in the name of Satan and in the name
of all demons, come just now to me, therefore I order you in the
name of the most holy trinity. . . . I order you to come to me
without delay, and send me another evil spirit which will help

me to accomplish what you want me to do and to help my will to carry it out.' What a prayer! These words illustrate the lengths to which the devil will go to keep a hold on his clients. This boy was deceived, because he did not receive anything except isolation from his community. He wanted to succeed at school in order to have a good job and be rich later, but all in vain. Today he is on the bottom rung of the ladder of life; he has to learn even how to live with others before he can think of earning a living.

When people come to tell me their stories they cannot believe that the devil will ever leave them alone. As they say themselves, 'We went too far, we spoke with the dead. We sat on the graves and saw human beings in the form of white ghosts. Do you really say that God can reverse the coin and consider me once more his beloved child?' I assure them that they will be accepted by God and that we shall offer them special divine protection. It is true that they went too far. There is no objection to having an ambition to become rich, but one must work for it using normal means. The consequences of using the help of the underworld are indeed terrible.

My friend in question, in spite of having offered himself to the devil, suffered from a mysterious and incurable disease. His farm business was in a shambles. He was at loggerheads with his wife. Everything went wrong except his work in a government ministry, but as time passed even that was threatened by his mysterious disease which no doctor managed to pinpoint and diagnose. He came to me almost against his own belief, but encouraged by a friend who had been delivered from the same club of the spirit-agents. He came with his family, was delivered from the evil one, and today he looks at life from a different viewpoint. He cannot believe that he is free. He is well and prosperous, and, what is more important, God is with him.

(*Plunging into Darkness*, pp. 1–8)

It took us more than two years to deliver a sixteen-year-old girl from twenty-five devils. The process was too long to describe here. This girl was first thought to be suffering from heart failure, and was brought to the hospital, where she was considered to be seriously ill. She would faint and was believed to be in a coma for some hours. Someone thought of us, and instead of transferring her to the Central Hospital they brought her to us.

For fifteen hours we were unable to communicate with her. She could not eat anything, her body was stiff and her eyes were closed. She was in another world, which we could not reach. We knew but one fact, that if it was God's will that instead of going to the Central Hospital she was directed to come to us, God would show us the way to deliver her from the evil spirits. At certain moments we were afraid that she would suddenly die, since it was not clear to us what the real matter was. We called the parents and some relatives and we all gathered in the room where she was. The mother began to speak to the spirits. What a terrifying experience. The answering voice came from the girl as clear as it could ever be. But one noticed at the same time that only the mouth was alive. It is a terrifying thing to look at, because one literally witnesses the presence of an entity in a body which is not its own. The entity, as it spoke, left the body as cold as it could ever be; there was no reaction on the face, and no flowing of blood as one expects in facial expressions. This body was completely under the control of the evil one. The spirits ordered the mother: 'Go and bring her elder sister, then we shall discuss the matter.' Her elder sister was 80 miles away from Lusaka. She had to be brought.

The history of the two girls was that both of them from the one family decided to become nuns. Among the twenty-five evil spirits was a grandmother who had died years back. The elder sister of the sick girl had been given the name of the grandmother, who did not want her to 'lose' her name by not marrying if she became a nun. So the spirits were having their revenge on both girls by disturbing them in various ways — with trances, heart palpitations, convulsions and abdominal pains. (Up to now they are still struggling to become nuns.)

Coming back to the sixteen-year-old girl, we spoke with the spirits and ordered them to leave the girl because they were parasites in her life. After a long struggle they told us that they were going out of her, but that they would wait for her at home, and this is what happened on several occasions. She would be delivered from them and as long as she remained with us, she would feel well, but on her return home she became miserable. On some occasions she would fall at the door of her parents' home, just as she was about to step inside. These were very difficult spirits to deal with, because they did not often speak to us or answer our questions.

Living in a world of gossip, the frequent appearances of this girl at our home did not bring us comfort. On the other hand we knew that the Lord was directing her to us, because she was certain that one day she would be healed. Several times we offered her to Jesus Christ by leaving her in a trance to spend the whole night in the chapel. She would wake up the next morning finding herself in the safe hands of the Lord. On some occasions we had the Exposition of the Blessed Sacrament for her, leaving the deliverance in the Lord's power. We felt on these occasions that our being instruments of the Lord had reached exhaustion, and so we had to go back to the One Who had commissioned us to deliver this girl from the evil one. One day, while in the chapel, we succeeded in speaking to the spirits, and by the authority of the Lord we ordered them to answer the questions: How many are you? What are your names? Why do you not obey the orders of the Lord? They answered that they were now only three remaining: Satan, the grandmother (or an evil spirit taking her name), and a nameless spirit. Satan told us that this girl was a pledge to them. They had healed her mother from mysterious diseases, and in her misery she had taken an oath that if Satan healed her she would give him her daughter for seven years. He said that he had been with her for only two years so far, and that it was not possible for them to leave her. They added that the girl was not behaving herself; she did not follow their instructions, especially because she was still thinking of becoming a nun. For this behaviour they had to continue torturing her. They repeated to us this revelation on another occasion, so we had no alternative but to call her mother. Then the spirits answered, 'We shall do all we can to prevent her from coming here.' She too, being under the control of the spirits, did not come to us. So we used the authority of the Lord to cut this pledge. Both the girls are now well, but we still feel that the mother must come to us and untie the oath before us. Then the girl will be completely healed.

How often have people blamed us for the ineffectiveness of our prayers while they know that they do not open themselves totally to us. Hence we have often obliged some of our patients to bring all the utensils and all the medicines they were given by the *sing'angas* (medicine men). If these things have failed to heal them and to deliver them from the evil spirits, we feel that they should be brought to us. We shall replace them with the power of the Lord in their lives, and with some sacramentals like holy water. One woman has refused to bring the utensils and the medicines, and the spirits have also forbidden her to enter the church. She has to make a choice between Jesus and Satan, but she is so afraid of the threat of death from Satan that she does not reflect on the victory of Jesus over sin, death and Satan himself. Nor does she believe in our protective devices if she should decide to return totally to the fold. It is not easy to persuade her. This is what happens when you make an oath with the devil: he will see to it that you keep it. It is easy to walk into the devil's chain, but hard to walk out of it.

(*Plunging into Darkness*, pp. 13–15)

Revelations from the devil

When listening to the messages from the ancestral spirits, all present can hear what they say. The questions asked make the language of the guardian (or benign) spirits simple and understandable. The people still consider the voice of the ancestor as something supernatural, and they keep the message with reverential fear, so the whole community is aware of the common need of living well together, depending on how each one abides by the advice of the ancestors.

But my aim here is not so much to speak of those ancestral spirits who are 'guardians' of the living, but rather of the evil spirits, who reveal many unknown facts concerning people and events. I call this a 'gift', not so much for its purpose, but rather for the fact that it comes to a person without effort. I have often spoken of 'agents' of the devil — i.e. trusted 'managers' who, while acting on his ultimate directions, can be left relatively free to carry out his work. This is a very important rank in the spirit world, because the devils are spirits and they can only operate in the physical world through someone or something physical. They have their own disciples, and in Zambia they even baptise them in the name of Satan. They go to the river, where the clients are washed and ordered to leave their old clothes by the river. They return home in new clothes. At night they are put to the test to see if they can dance. From the way one dances the spirit is known as a lion, a snake, a chief, or a foreign one. The spirits speak different languages according to what they are. A lion will roar, a monkey will howl, a snake will hiss, Sung'uni will speak the Nsenga-Luzi language perfectly, a Chewa will speak Bemba, and so forth. (Sung'uni is the chief serpent devil among the Nsenga-Luzi people.)

Speaking languages does not mean speaking in tongues, though it is true that the devil speaks in tongues. Here I am speaking of a possessed person who, for instance, speaks five languages — so well that the listener cannot know the mother-tongue of the possessed. I was recently taken aback by one woman who had five spirits: a Portuguese, a Canadian, a Bemba, a Nsenga-Luzi, and a snake. This woman changed from Portuguese to English, from English to Bemba, from Bemba to Nsenga with such ease, and spoke the languages so perfectly, that she almost drew away my attention from sending away the spirits. I was astounded to the core. And she is such a simple woman when she is normal. What a pity that some people cannot believe it, or will rather say that these languages come from the subconscious self, which may be traced back to hidden experiences of babyhood. They mean to say that no one can speak a language so perfectly on the spur of the moment without previous study of it. But what I have described is a fact, and I have heard of many more cases.

Revelations from evil spirits are very disturbing, which is why casting out demons is not easy for an unprepared person, who will be shocked at being known by the devils. And of course if the one casting out demons happens to be controlled by them, they will protect that person from being exposed as a liar. They will say, for instance, 'What do you want to do — cast us out? You, who are subject to us?' They know exactly the extent of their kingdom. The things they say may be true, and may also not be true; to the listeners it will be extremely hard not to believe what the spirits say.

It is wise to take serious precautions in casting out devils. I have heard of a very reputable priest, who dared on his own to cast out demons. He exhausted himself for nothing, and I think that the devils knew that he was just experimenting his presumed power on the possessed. Recently in Kenya I also heard of a priest who failed completely to cast out demons; the ordinary faithful as a group came together, prayed over the possessed and cast the devils out.

Do the things which the devils speak about materialise? Yes, they do. They may speak of things which happen in a community, or which will happen. They also threaten to take certain steps against the one who is casting them out. They have often told me that they would kill the possessed. I remain calm and tell them that life is in God's hands, and therefore their would-be victim will live. One day, when I was contending with them in a possessed woman, they said to me: 'Who are you? Don't you know that we have power to lift you up?' I assured them that they could not lift me up. Then I asked them: 'Who are you?' The answer came: 'I am the devil. This one is mine. I shall not go away.' Boastfully the devil turned the possessed to me and changed her face into a hollow-like shape, with the eyes pulled inside, and the forehead and the mouth as if they were going to be folded up and joined together. It was a terrible sight. I had with me a man and a lady in the room. I had told them to say the rosary to back me up, which is very important at such crucial moments in the lives of the possessed. The force of the voice of the devil and the tone of refusal as he said 'This one is mine; I shall not go away' put the two into confusion. One did not have a rosary and when the other found hers, they pulled it apart with their fear as they stretched it to find a place to hold it in order to begin to pray. Up to this day I do not know whether they began with the recitation of the Creed, or with the Our Father. When they tell the story themselves, one gets even more confused than I was myself that time. The one fact which consoled me was that they both took hold of a rosary. To see the devil in a human form is a horrible sight, and their confusion is more than understandable. However, their prayers helped me to send away the ugly creature, and today the woman is a beauty with her normal features.

The devils often say things which are true, but one should not base one's actions on such casual or occasional prophecies, which give the devil himself the opportunity to become one's regular counsellor and source of information. He always prophesies for his own interests. Some Christian exorcists have considered themselves enriched by knowledge obtained from the devil during exorcism, and in the mean time forgot that they were to be on duty and supposed to be sending him out of the possessed. One must be calm as one listens to these prophecies. Some of them turn out to be complete lies, but sometimes when he boasts of doing harm, he can do it. It is not good to allow him to do what he wants to do to the possessed. They bang themselves on the floor, pull out their hair from their head, squeeze their stomachs or crawl on the floor like snakes. The devils showed me one day how they could deflect an act of exorcism that way by suddenly afflicting the possessed with a fit of epilepsy. They did it so quickly that I had no time to forestall it. However, I managed to bring the victim back to normal.

A status in society as an agent

To be an agent of the devil is a rank which cannot be disputed. In a society like ours today, which is full of hatred, gossip, economic competition and jealousy, the devil comes in as a great protector to a person. In the mean time he hides himself in all those ills which befall society. For instance, those possessed by the devil will fight tooth and nail against all those human beings who are witches (needless to say the devil is causing as much harm in society as the witches). The reason why the witches will be revealed by the possessed is because there is no place for two kingdoms in the one they have possessed. Another reason may be that the power of a witch is just a share of the power which is inherent in the devil. For this reason the devil poses as superior to a witch. A possessed person in a trance can point out a witch and his victims, and can even go so far as to show the audience the hidden places where the witch puts his medicines.

What I found out from experience is that there is no unity among those in the devil's kingdom. They work like hungry wolves all of which know when they see a reindeer that it will provide meat for them. So they all close in together and when they have caught it, each eats whatever it can get, without thinking of the others. So too the devils know that human beings are the ones left with a free choice, and they will not leave them free till they have pulled many to their side. In this operation there is no order and no unity. The devil has no sense of obedience, even if from time to time one tells us, 'Satan has sent us here.'

When therefore we speak of agents of the devils, these are able, as human beings, to be subject to the devil because they are still human. Human nature is subject to God but it can be persuaded otherwise. This goodness in humanity, together with awareness of being subject to someone, prepares the way for the devil, who tries to sway a human being according to his own whims. With many promises, he gives assurance that all will be well. He has tempted many people to be healers, while he himself inflicts many diseases. He does not heal, but only deceives people by using something like what I may call spiritual sedatives giving temporary release from one spot which was diseased, which then continues to give the same pain somewhere else. This victim believes that he or she was healed from dizziness some days back and now suffers only from headaches. In the meantime the agent receives quantities of money, and having power to diagnose diseases beyond ordinary knowledge, enjoys a position in the community inspiring both respect and fear. If the disease comes from human hands, the agent of the devil will say so in clear terms, and sometimes even tell the patient exactly when the sickness began. Thus many think of devils' agents as divine: it is believed that they share the knowledge, hidden from the majority, which God has about us.

How does one become an agent of the devil? It is hard for me to discuss personal motives for doing so. I shall restrict myself to those who answer to this precise description, and not speak of those who sound as if their clan spirits give them a mandate to be priests in their families, or of those who join the devil's club, but speak rather of those who actually share his powers and can display them at will. In order to share the devil's powers they have to get rid of what is called by the master of ceremonies a spirit which is incompatible with their own. They pray over the patient. They ask him to isolate himself from others. They give him medicine to be drunk at odd times, such as 'before flies begin to move about', i.e. before dawn, and after the witches have stopped roaming about and have gone to bed. The reason why this time is important is that if the patient drinks medicine when the witches are still going about bewitching people, that medicine will lose its curative power. The witches are believed to neutralise the medicine.

An agent of the devil is usually a lonely person. The agent has to eat specific foods selected by the spirits, use special vessels which should be used by no one else, and wear special clothes as a sign of office. Some of them, from the day they become the devil's agents, are not allowed to live with their wives or husbands; they are married to the spirits just as, ideally, many in the priesthood and the religious life for the sake of the Kingdom give up natural marriage and are married to Christ. It is already somehow an impossible task to bring back to the fold an agent of the devil, someone who is married to the evil spirits. To think of it makes my body shudder. This way of life is no consecration in the way we understand it but rather a union with the devil which is beyond ordinary possession. It is a complete sharing of self with the devil. The devil himself ties the bond of wedlock, and to his agent he will give anything, and allow him or her to display all kinds of signs and strange things.

On the day of approval the neophyte, after passing through the necessary conditions, is told to expect the message from the devil during the night. At night the devil comes in different forms. He may come with a rod, which means that this person will be a teacher or a preacher. He or she may also have the power to choose Bible texts, suitable for preaching (as the devil did in the wilderness to tempt Jesus), and may be presented with white clothes and roots, which are the signs of a healer. These signs are well known to the instructors. On waking up, the neophyte must explain to the instructors what happened during the night, and will then be told what his or her specific vocation and role as the devil's agent will be.

One may be tempted to lose hope and think that the evil one is winning, but not everything is in his power. Even the fact that we know so much about him shows that he is losing. Listen to the promise of the Lord: 'In that day, the Lord with his hard and great and strong sword will punish Leviathan the fleeing serpent, Leviathan the twisting serpent, and he will slay the dragon that is in the sea' (Isaiah 27.1). It cost the blood of Jesus, His Son, to possess the human race totally once more. The time has come when the devil must realise that the fold of the sheep is guarded and is well protected. The Holy Spirit is coming to the fore to reaffirm and continue the work of Jesus. The evil one has to give way, and he is giving way.

(*Plunging into Darkness*, pp. 18–24)

To the would-be exorcist

How often we ourselves have sincerely said, 'Certainly, the finger of God is here. I can't pinpoint what has changed this man or this woman in the few words we have exchanged in the Confessional.' Thousands of souls have found their way back to God through a few minutes of Confession of their sins to a priest. Though the formula used in the sacrament of Confession does not directly expel the evil one, the mention of deliverance from sins is genuinely an exercise of exorcism. In the old formula there were two most important elements of exorcism. One was '*Dominus noster Jesus Christus te absolvat. . . .*' (May the Lord Jesus Christ deliver you). The simple meaning is 'May the Lord Jesus Christ loosen you or untie you. . . .' This had a very deep meaning, if only the penitent understood what the priest was saying. The second element makes a priest recognise his role as a minister of Christ, and so he relies on the authority of Jesus Christ and concludes by delivering a penitent in the name of the Trinity: '*Et ego autoritate sua te absolvo a peccatis tuis in nomine Patris et Filii et Spiritus Sancti, Amen.*' Those who formulated this prayer of deliverance from sins understood that the battle against the powers of darkness has to be won as we fight together with Christ, not by going it alone.

In the sacrament of Baptism many priests have experienced the direct reaction of the presence of the evil one with his companions in the many adults they baptise. There have been cases of catechumens who trembled or fell down as they were receiving Baptism. Even ordinary people took these signs as facts of deliverance from evil spirits. In the old rite the priest repeated the formula of exorcism more than three times, and used direct language against the evil one. He finally confirmed it by the public confession of those to be baptised by declaring that they have decided to follow Jesus. They said: 'I reject Satan and all his works and pomps . . .' Then they declared as well that they believed in the Holy Trinity, the Catholic Church and the Communion of Saints. In these two sacraments, of Baptism and Penance, a minister of religion has by ordination the power to deliver people from evil spirits.

The danger of presumption

Let me stress from the outset the presumptuous angle of exorcism which may lead many ordained ministers on to spiritual precipices. The word 'presumption' here does not mean that a priest assumes for himself powers which he does not have. No! It only means that he may have the same easy disposition to expel evil spirits, which he has when dealing with the avowed catechumens who are being baptized. I am now alluding to dealing with evil spirits outside the two sacraments of Penance and Baptism.

I call the exercise of deliverance in these two sacraments 'easy', and I mean it, but this 'being easy' does not mean that the results are in any way cheap. What I mean is that a priest is engaged on his ordinary duty and is dealing with the people who are co-operating with him in many ways. It is true that sometimes he comes across a hardened sinner. However, he is still consoled to know that that person has come on his/her own to Confession or is willing to be baptised. I would say that the battle is already half won. The penitent and the catechumen have already within themselves the will to fight evil and to reject it. In the case of Baptism the preparations have been going on for many years. So one can safely say: 'The evil one and his companions are being weakened step by step.' The evil spirits are certainly aware that they are in the wrong place, and that there is a battle being waged against them, even though it advances at a slow pace during each year of the catechumenate. The picture I have of deliverance in the sacraments of Baptism and Penance is one of a drowning person who cries for help and people run to the rescue, and that person co-operates with them. The picture I have of deliverance outside the sacraments is that of someone in the claws of a lion, say under the lion's legs, who cries for help. Though people may want to help, they have to take the utmost precautions. It is not enough to be courageous to face the lion, but one must also be prepared to die for the one who is under its claws. Yet one must use all possible means not to rouse the lion to such a rage that it may lead to the complete destruction of the one who is supposed to be delivered. That is why I strongly feel that many ministers of religion have had presumptions as they faced the evil spirits outside the sacraments. It is not an iron will which sends away the devil which has come to settle in a person, but rather the power of Christ which flows into the one who is engaged in the battle to establish His Kingdom.

It is not giving merit to the devil to say that he is intelligent and powerful. He is, and it is a fact. He has both physical and spiritual powers. Today he is controlling some people who have great public reputation. He has covered them with other people's trust and confidence, and with these in their hands they have harmed thousands of innocent people. I have under my fingertips the shocking stories of the hypocrisy of some men and women in the sanctuary, who are completely under the control of the devil; I was told somewhere in Europe that as they preach one is able to know in whom they believe by their gestures. In many places in Europe it is believed that the devil was put to death by the resurrection of Christ. But the fact is that he is risen and is living in quite a few of them — to put it mildly. The devil is not always known by such names as Hansaan, Ngoza, Roam, Chibwe and Nabaroth. No, not at all. Sometimes he is known as Laziness, Dumbness, Epilepsy, Sloth, Lust, Alcoholism, Pride or Lies. Those who are waiting to see the devil in the form of a reptile again will have to wait a long time, till Adam and Eve go back to Eden. Today the devil puts on coats of many different colours.

There is no doubt at all that some people and even priests have their fixed expectations of the shape of the devil, and of the symptoms and reactions he produces in a person. But in reality, because the devil is intelligent, he does not act according to fixed patterns, as if by instinct. He makes decisions, and adapts his plans to every situation and to the person who is the target. The devil known in our language as chief devil of the waters is Sung'uni. To women he takes the form of a man who comes to propose marriage. To men he may come in the form of a woman without a head, whose face cannot be recognised. These are the devils of lust. These victims, men and women, undergo terrible tortures in their reproductive systems, with the result that many of them have been incapacitated in their marital relations with their spouses. I dealt with a man who could no longer be a husband to his wife, with the consequence that she abandoned him. After suffering for thirteen years he came to me, and I must say that when one is delivering these people from the devil of lust, it is the most shocking sight one can see. Though this man was finally delivered from the evil one after thirteen years, he had no way at hand to have his wife back, who by then was remarried.

Equally, because of fixed ideas and beliefs with regard to the shape of the devil and his ways of dealing with people, a minister may send away a reptile when the devil is alcoholism. Then the devil laughs when he knows that he is being missed. I have often heard the many devils in one person accusing one another of having caused the different diseases in that person. They say: 'It is Chibwe who is in the chest.' 'We have been sent by Juma from Tanga.' 'Sung'uni has married her and does not want her to be touched by her husband.' 'No, I am not Satan.' Then we ask: 'Who are you?' And answer comes: 'I am Mulenga the chief.' There are very few evil spirits which have not taken names. They know that names mean more than words in identifying a person, and that a name *means* a person. Hence they often take noble names, names of chiefs and of famous men and women, or they identify themselves with power, through a strong animal like a lion. In the hierarchy of evil spirits there are also what we may call minor spirits. There may be many of these, identifying themselves with simple people or animals, like hyenas, snakes or well-known birds. The greatest lie one comes across in dealing with evil spirits is the way they also identify themselves with famous dead relatives. Beginners in the ministry of deliverance will believe this the first time they experience it, but often in the course of deliverance one discovers that the evil spirits are great liars. At a later stage they confess that they are bad angels, or bad people who have just taken this or that name so that the relatives may give them all the honour they used to give to their beloved dead.

I was partly happy and partly sad when I read the following in P. Van Pelt's book *Bantu Customs* (on mainland Tanzania): 'There is thus much confusion and there are no clear-cut ideas about the spirits. The best seems to be to consider separately the ancestor-spirits and the other mysterious beings in whose existence the Bantu believe.' To those who have not dealt with the spirits there is confusion if their knowledge has been acquired by oral and written research. The means which we use to know the category to which a spirit belongs is the penetrating power of Jesus which disturbs the evil spirits and forces them to confess who they are: 'I tell you all this that in me you may find peace. You will suffer in the world. But take courage! I have overcome the world' (John 16.33). We must take the words of Jesus literally: He *has* overcome the world and He continues to overcome the world in every era, but through human beings.

Spiritual diplomats

In today's world the fear of the enemy is in itself a superstition, which has made some religious ministers become spiritual diplomats. They have accepted somehow a co-existence with the enemy, the devil. They say he is not there, and when they are told that he is there, they tell the possessed that they should believe that he is not there. So the truth should logically be as follows: 'I believe in God. . . . in Jesus Christ. . . . in the Holy Spirit . . .' and never mention the existence of the enemy who made the life of Jesus so difficult while He lived among us. Through the force of evil, which is manifested in the actions of evil people, we must believe that there is an existing spring which actually generates evil, namely the devil. Hence Jesus says to His ministers: 'If the world hates you, know that it has hated me before it hated you. If you were of the world, the world would love its own; but because you are not of the world, and I chose you out of the world, therefore the world hates you' (John 15.18–19). The religious diplomats do not want to be hated by today's world. That is why they avoid anything that hurts the world, and in the mean time they deny the full powers Jesus has given them to overcome the world. The world at issue is the enemy of Christ. In this context 'to be of the world' means to belong to a group of evil people, 'full of malice and pride', the agents of the devil and the devil himself. Hence Jesus says elsewhere, 'If I had not come, if I had not spoken to them, they would have been blameless; but as it is they have no excuse for their sin' (John 15.22). What I want to point out here is that the enemies of Christ are a reality and not imaginary. The religious minister must take it upon himself to fight the evil which exists in the world, and which prevents the growth to spiritual adulthood of the followers of Christ.

Victory over Satan

Why do we not come out clearly and show that we are here to fight Satan and his agents? There has never been an era after Christ's descent on earth, or His ascent to heaven, when Satan did not exist. Jesus precisely came to fight Satan and to win us back from him. What Jesus did was to assure us that He overcame death, sin and Satan. He did it on our behalf and gave us all the means to do the same, provided that we imitate His life and reproduce it in ourselves. He wants us also on our own to overcome sin, death and Satan. He assures us of the victory in the following words, which He spoke to the apostles: 'You are already made clean by the word which I have spoken to you. Abide in me and I in you. As the branch cannot bear fruit by itself, unless it abides in the vine, neither can you unless you abide in me. I am the vine, you are the branches' (John 15.3−5). If as ministers of religion we have truly lived in the vine, which is Jesus, we should have no fear of the enemy, not even to mention him by name. Satan existed even when Jesus Christ walked on this earth. We read the following: 'And in the synagogue there was a man who had the spirit of an unclean demon; and he cried out with a loud voice, "Ah! What have you to do with us, Jesus of Nazareth? Have you come to destroy us? I know who you are, the Holy One of God." But Jesus rebuked him saying, "Be silent and come out of him!" And when the demon had thrown him down in the midst, he came out of him, having done him no harm. And they were all amazed and said to one another: "What is this word? For with authority and power he commands the unclean spirits, and they come out" ' (Luke 4. 33−6).

Let us forget about being spiritual diplomats. Satan will not give us a dime even if we are polite to him. He laughs at our lack of confidence in the merits of redemption, and our lack of confidence in the power of Jesus. Father John Hardon seems to put it well in the article in his book *Holiness in the Church* which is entitled 'Christ our strength'. He begins by asking the following question: 'Why, we ask, does Christ so often remind us to be brave, not to falter, to be courageous?' In the answer to this question Father Hardon analyses the different fears which are often hidden behind our religious diplomacy: '[It is] because He knew that our greatest obstacle to serving Him as we should is fear — fear of the opposition that loyalty to Jesus always brings

in its wake; fear of the indifference of those whom we have come
to love, or, as Christ put it, the enemies in our own household;
and above all fear of ourselves, whom we know all too well and
by whom we have been so often betrayed.'
(*Precautions in the Ministry of Deliverance*, pp. 3–6, 11–12)

[In the above passages Milingo does not see the evil spirits as African
spirits. Rather they are universal, and to be found in the Bible. If he is
rather ambiguous as to whether they incorporate human vices or are
persons in their own right, perhaps this is because he finds them so
ambiguous. Certainly his personification of them sounds strange, and
may be hard for Westerners to accept. However, one thing is clear,
namely that he is pointing to power which the Church has been given
and has always possessed, but is failing to use — wasted power. His
appeal to exorcists to be patient and gentle shows that he understands
this power as the power of love, of God who is love. Some of the
sufferers he treats may never in their whole lives have experienced
love. Someone who had been a patient in the neurology ward of a great
hospital expressed amazement at the patience and lovingness of the
staff, which had results in bringing back to life minds apparently lost
through brain damage. That kind of nursing is more than medicine
and is close to what the Church is capable of. It is certain that Milingo
speaks from experience which is beyond the ordinary.]

God is on our side

It sounds so religious to be known as someone who is prudent,
even if in such people there may be selfishness and pride. The
treasurer of a charitable organisation may be called prudent if
he controls the funds of the organisation to such an extent that
there will always be something remaining in the bag. On the
other hand the reason behind it may be that he merely hates to
beg on behalf of the organisation, and the result is that he sends
away many clients saying that he has no funds to help them. In
the history of the organisation he will be known as a generous
person, though not extravagant. He enjoyed being known as
prudent, although he let many people suffer who were entitled
to the funds which he was holding back, and should not have
suffered while the funds were available to release them from
their misery. There are many religious ministers who enjoy a
good reputation in the Church, while they spend very little of
God's gifts in the service of the people of God. There is a story of

a man who was said to have passed through life with an incredible integrity, about whom it was said that 'he was not touched by the briars of the forest', meaning that he made no mistake in life. Someone answered: 'He never passed through the forest', meaning that he did nothing on earth, which was why he made no mistake. He was very prudent! Many of us like to keep our good name rather than plunge into what are known as demanding situations. I appeal to my fellow-ministers of religion to consider their work as something to be spent, and not to keep the gifts of God in reserve. They are treasurers of God's gifts, and by His own order they must dish them out to the holy people of God. 'I have come that they may have life and have it more abundantly' (John 10.10). Father Hardon comments: 'In pursuit of this goal, He preached and He lived, He suffered and He died. He has invited us to share in this enterprise in the Catholic Church under His Vicar. We are to extend His Kingdom to the ends of the earth — the catholicity of space. We are to teach without adulteration, in all its evangelical quality, His message, unchanged, the same that He taught in Palestine — the catholicity of time' (*Holiness in the Church*).

In the realm of exorcism we need to confess Christ and His power. We are living in the era of the Holy Spirit, and this is the power Christ promised us to enable us to go through the forest of life without being driven back: 'I send down upon you the promise of my Father. Remain here in the city until you are clothed with power from on high' (Luke 24.49). In the Acts of the Apostles Jesus clearly states what this power is: 'You will receive power when the Holy Spirit comes down on you; then you are to be my witnesses in Jerusalem, throughout Judea and Samaria, yes, even to the ends of the earth' (Acts 1.8).

Being watched from a distance

We are living in an age in which the devil challenges the power of Jesus. He knows that he has no foothold in the human race as a whole, since Jesus challenged and vanquished him. But he knows that there are still millions of people who don't know what Jesus has done for them, and what he has gained for them, as a means to overcome the devil and his agents. It is our duty to teach people the work of redemption, and give away what we have in our spiritual savings. We shall rejoice to see so many sick people having access to these spiritual savings. In the ministry of deliverance, we have been obliged to teach people a simple formula which has not always been a success: 'Jesus, heal me. Jesus, I love you. In Jesus' Name I send you away, you Satan.' We aim at involving the sick person in the deliverance. However, since it sounds like an emergency device, the devil in some cases is so strong that he does not allow the person to utter the name 'Jesus'. On the one hand the devil knows the power of the name 'Jesus', on the other the patients do not thoroughly grasp the nature of its power. However, many who make the effort come out victorious. The patients must believe in the power of the Blood of Jesus, and at moments like these during the ministry of deliverance, they must co-operate by confessing Jesus. Hence we read in Revelations: 'And they overcame him [Satan] by the Blood of the Lamb, and the word of their testimony' (Rev. 12.11). This is what Don Basham calls 'practising "pleading the Blood" '. He advises Christians as follows: 'This is an ancient form of asking for divine protection; it entails claiming our rights as Christians to be protected from the Evil One. Jesus defeated Satan by going to the cross and shedding His Blood. We can claim the victory for ourselves' (*Deliver us from Evil*).

Are we being watched from a distance? Whatever may be the case, God is on our side. What we need is more than just an abstract faith; we need a living faith. For a long time Satan took to himself the honour of being considered clever, and he made many people believe that he is so clever that we cannot know many of the tactics he uses in his destructive work among the people of God. Today there are thousands of people who have dealt directly with him and many have written about their experience with him and his agents. It is hard to say who is watching whom. We do not underestimate his power, but it is far weaker than that of Jesus, who is our Lord and Saviour. Hence we are warned by the Vatican Council II in the following words: 'A monumental struggle against the powers of darkness pervades the whole history of man. The battle was joined from the very origins of the world and will continue until the last day, as the Lord has attested. Caught in this conflict, man is obliged to wrestle constantly if he is to cling to what is good, *nor can he achieve his own integrity without great efforts and the help of*

God's grace' (Vatican Council II, *Constitution on the Church in the Modern World*, III. 37). We have stressed those last words.

I was edified to hear a priest confess: 'We have become functionaries. We are just administrators in our parishes.' This was Europe, not Zambia. This statement sounds sweeping, and it might have been true of him as an individual. What interested me was the acknowledgement that he had fallen below the expected standard of what a priest should be. Certainly a priest who is capable of administering his parish only as an organiser, without the spirit of Christ in his work, should not dare to embark on the ministry of deliverance. Who knows what concept he has of the importance of time, when he plans everything in that framework, and values every minute. He calculates how long the deliverance will take according to the number of people present and how long it takes to work on each one. I would strongly advise anyone who has such an attitude to steer clear of the ministry of deliverance, which is rather achieved by 'great efforts and the help of God's grace', not merely by measuring out time and by good planning. The devil will easily follow the thought-process of such a one, and will bring him to the realisation that other things are more important than deliverance, and make him say, reasonably, that one person may be sacrificed in order to serve many who are not touched by this psychic disease! In this case the devil will certainly be watching him from a distance. He will notice the ebbing of his fervour in prayer, as he looks at his watch — one hour, two hours, what a waste of time. He orders the devil to go away, not so much by the authority of Jesus, but by his own authority and by the use of anger and harsh words; he no longer pays attention to the value and meaning of the words he uses. At this stage he is quarrelling with the devil, which is what the devil wanted him to do. If any one engages in a duel with Satan he will lose it, because he is using his own efforts without the help of God's grace. In the realm of exorcism we human beings are not standing in the ordinary arena. We are in the world of the spirits, and so in order to stand firm and face the enemy, we need to be clothed properly — hence the need of God's grace. We understand why the astronauts who went to the moon needed special food, special clothes and special breathing equipment; the moon is another world not fit for man to live in. Hence we too need something unusual in order to face our enemy on his own battle-field.

The fault of impatience

I must confess that I hate to see anger, although I am myself subject to the same vice. I cannot stand seeing someone being shouted at, and humiliated by harsh words. My feelings are with those of Moses, when he saw his fellow-Jew being ill-treated by an Egyptian; except that I cannot go as far as Moses in committing murder.

Let me come to 'the impatience of the minister' in the ministry of deliverance. I have watched the dryness of the service itself, which reflects the 'functionary' side of the minister. I have watched the patients being tossed to and fro like helpless epileptics. It shocked me to see them being treated so carelessly as if they were of little account. In this atmosphere I feel that it is out of place to call upon the name of Jesus, who was Himself 'meek and humble of heart'. Watching all the manoeuvres in the ministry of deliverance, I would not take part in what I call a demonstration of power. Is it surprising then that often such ministers have only disturbed the evil spirits, but without sending them away? In this case the warning of Niccolo Machiavelli in *The Prince* should be appropriate: 'An enemy offended, and left to live a second day, becomes an enemy twice over.' These evil spirits who have only been disturbed presume that they have rather overcome their enemy. They may use the same tactics to provoke the next minister to anger or to a mere demonstration of power. Why get angry with the possessed? Why get angry with the devil?

I felt so sorry that in the film *The Exorcist* the two priests lost the battle. I understood every detail of that film; it was as if I had taken part in it. I anticipated the reaction of the devil, whom I was watching from a distance. The life of the young priest was far from what is expected of an exorcist; he was a modern priest, and seemed to me to have been serious only when he was on duty. When he found the older priest dead, he got furious and began beating the possessed girl. The devil went into him and threw him out through the window, and he died. The girl was delivered, but one wonders why the devil left the girl, or whether he actually left her for good. If he did, by whose authority was it? There was no guarantee for her security; as she regained her consciousness she felt helpless because those who were supposed to receive her into her new life had both died in the course of her deliverance. Thus the story is very incomplete.

No, it is not enough to have jurisdiction to exorcise the possessed, nor is it enough to recite a quantity of prayers of exorcism from the ritual. In today's world of Christian renewal there are some who may believe that they have been favoured with the gift of the ministry of deliverance. I accept that this may be considered a starting-point, but do not believe that they have automatic power to deliver someone from evil spirits. Personal dispositions are also very important. Anyone who works in the name of Jesus will be required, if called to the ministry, to pass through trials for personal purification, knowing that it is being done in the name of Jesus, who has a right to the possession of human beings; but no human being has the right to possess a fellow-human being. It is Jesus who overcame Satan and won back the human race for the glory of His Father. He says: 'Behold I have given you authority to tread upon serpents and scorpions, and over all the power of the enemy; and nothing shall hurt you. Nevertheless do not rejoice in this, that the spirits are subject to you, but rejoice that your names are written in heaven' (Luke 10. 19–20).

Humility

This matter of personal dispositions should not be misunderstood. We should never feel that we deserve the appointment from Jesus Christ to carry out this special duty. No! What I mean is that when Jesus calls us, we must be humble, and search for what he demands from us. From the outset it will be humility which will lead us to know who we are and what we are before God. We must have complete filial love for God, confirmed by the actual belief that He created us and is the first to have loved us. That Jesus Christ was sent to save us after the fall of the human race emphasises again the love God has for us as human beings. The role of Jesus is best appreciated when one acknowledges that we deserved eternal punishment. If Jesus identified Himself with our cause of misery and uprooted it, it was purely from a love which was not at that time reciprocal. He loved us so much, us who did not deserve to be loved and were incapable of loving. The mystery of God's love lay in the sacrifice of His own Son to give life to those who were dead, and to teach them to be divine, to become true children of God, who will have the right to enjoy eternal life.

The love of Jesus is extended even after His ascent to Heaven. He was not satisfied with only being with us in the Eucharist. He wanted us to grow into him also by knowing that in our day-to-day activities we should encounter the presence of the Holy Spirit. Jesus' words 'I am always with you' therefore become a reality through the presence of the Holy Spirit. As we carry out the work of deliverance, we must be aware of our instrumentality. Any speck of pride in our attitude towards the possessed, any hint of pride in our words, will weaken the power in us to carry out our duty to deliver our brothers and sisters from the evil spirits. To avoid all these human elements in this special work we need to become permanent habitations of the Holy Trinity.

This is how we are uplifted in the spiritual battlefield, and hence we can truly say that we have a spiritual bullet-proof uniform, the Presence of God within us. We do not need to get angry with the possessed, nor with the devil. The power of God within us and the authority of Jesus will do it all.

One day I was invited by a parish priest to pray over the sick. We went into the church. I was happy to have a companion in prayer. To my surprise, when the actual healing session began, my companion was not with me. He was far from me, making himself available for bringing holy water and the crucifix, and other small needs. He did not feel safe working with me, especially because among the patients there were some who were possessed. I have always felt so good when accompanied by my fellow-priests; we became strong in our prayers as a unit of four or five — the more the better. It was hard for me to force my friend to stand beside me. I know that he felt more secure doing the humble tasks, probably convinced that he was unworthy and was thus being humble. If only he had known how I needed him at that critical moment.

What I want to point out here is that, as a priest, he believed in what I was doing; he held to the Apostles' Creed with all the articles outlined in it. But I do not think he believed in the actualisation of the words of Jesus, 'Go out of him', as he commanded the devil to leave the possessed. We must actualise our faith by making it live; we did not receive the faith merely as a deposit in our souls, to exist in us alone. Faith is meant to make the deeds of Jesus come alive in us as we spend our lives as Christians. We cannot be Christians unless we actually live as Christians. And we cannot live as Christians unless we actualise the directives and principles of faith which Jesus left to guide us as we live in this world.

A carpenter needs the basic knowledge of his profession in order to practise it — the name and use of each tool, and the kind of wood he has to use for different kinds of articles. And his profession demands that his knowledge should be manifested in the beauty of the furniture he makes. Customers will conclude from this chair, that table and that drawer that the carpenter knows his job. We should expect the same of a Christian, especially a minister of religion, that his life should reflect a living faith. In the ministry of deliverance we need to be in a direct and living contact with God. The possessed must feel the presence of God, and the evil spirits must feel as well the powerful presence of Jesus, as we use His authority in deliverance and in the ministry of healing in general. We should all, as Christians, have this living faith. Cardinal Suenens confirms this in his book *The New Pentecost*: 'Each member of the Church is called to bear witness to his faith, both within the Church and outside it, and to actualise the potentialities conferred upon him in his baptism.'

Demands on personal life

Someone told me that my experience is a human experience, and that it should not be presented to readers as if it were as important as the Bible. I have no ambition to be a St Paul, a St Luke or a St John. However, my experience is a fact, and in many ways it is strange even to myself. It may be that it deserves to be described as 'human' experience because I am undoubtedly human, but I believe that it helps people to become divine and supernatural and closer to their Father in Heaven. It is intended to prove to them that their Father in

Heaven cares for them, and that He loves them, and wishes them happiness, joy, good health, peace, love and a life of harmony as true children of God. God is good, and God is love. In this ministry of deliverance and healing, the cure goes beyond the physical. Many people have come to believe more deeply in the existence of God. We rejoice with those who have not merely passed through a human experience, but who in the end have met God, and come closer to Him than they were before they attended a healing session.

At this point I am speaking to the individual minister of deliverance. It is true that the knife which is used to cut bread does not need to be sharpened as often as that which cuts meat, bones, vegetables and such things. However, the bread has a hard crust and depending on how often the knife is used in the family, it needs to be sharpened from time to time. I may be wrong in presuming that some who have the gift for the ministry of deliverance take the attitude of the knife that cuts bread, which remains forever sharp since it does not meet the same resistance as the meat knife. Such a one may believe that the evil spirits become as soft as the inside of a loaf of bread before him because he has the gift of deliverance. He may believe that he needs nothing more than this gift, which sets him on fire, to prepare himself for the ministry. He will say: 'God cannot contradict himself. He has given the gift plus the sustenance.' What a poor attitude! The logical conclusion of such a belief is that it will be God who will be blamed when, in the long run, the minister fails to carry out the ministry of deliverance. We may go farther than that and take the whole work of redemption as something which would be better appreciated if Jesus had done it to the full. This would mean that He should have finally caused us to be cleansed from sin and locked in Paradise for everlasting life. No, when He imparts the gift He wants it to be used for the community, but He expects that everything in us should be alerted to the presence of the gift and co-operate with its demands in order that it may be used to the full. One would not feel safe carrying a gun as a defence against lions in the forest if one did not know how to use it. One must learn how to aim properly and which part of the lion to shoot at in order to kill it, and above all one must have the courage to face an angry lion. The gifts which God gives us are to be used for the purposes God has in mind. But they can only be used to the extent that we co-operate with the demands of the gifts. The man who is facing a lion is the actual person who kills it; we do not say that the gun has killed the lion. *He* has killed the lion with the gun, and we call him a brave man. God had a reason for giving certain gifts to certain people. He does not expect them to be buried; they have to be used and bear fruit. If they are not used properly, we shall have to answer for them, and if they are abused we may even be punished. Let us respond to the call before us to continue His services to the people He redeemed. All these gifts complete the work of Jesus for the salvation of mankind.

How often we put God to shame with our behaviour. We take His gifts as if they had originated in us. We assume for ourselves the honour we gain from them, and we would like to let people know how rare they are, as if to say that we too are rare among human beings. We explain the gifts as if they were new mysteries found under the ocean, and we desire to be put into a museum as beings to be admired but not touched. I am certain that God does not give us these gifts in order that we may be treated like gold. If we have to use them for the community, we should be members of the community, and not be treated as something extraordinary. I once listened to someone relating to me that he had performed a miracle, and knew that it was not a miracle and was something that would have happened anyhow. He had cheapened himself for he had no fear of the One who had solved the riddle of life on the death-bed of the patient. Life is in the hands of God, not man. How dare one say 'I brought someone back to life', if that person was truly dead, without being filled with awe? There is a need for balance in all that we do in the name of God.

The respect we have in Africa for the visitors who come to us is reflected in all the ways in which we treat them. Watch our mothers, they do not use the same vessels for food when an exalted person visits us. When we are alone in the family it may be a young girl who brings food to the table. But when this noble visitor takes a meal with us, it will be the mother herself who sets the table and will use the best plates, which are immaculately clean. The food has to be first-class. All this is done as a sign to acknowledge the dignity of the visitor. You may say that it is only the words of politeness that matter, but it is not true. The whole atmosphere must reflect the respect and reverence we have for our special visitor.

One wonders, by contrast, at how careless gifted people sometimes are as they put their God-given gifts to use. To appreciate the value of the divine gift, it is important to handle it with care in acknowledgement of the great favour God has given us; the way we use it, and the scruples we have as we use it, will reflect the reverence and respect we have for the Donor. If we truly realise that the gifts we have come from God, we should live up to what God would like to see in those whom He has chosen to carry out certain missions to His people. It may happen that a person with gifts of healing may cure people even when drunk, but one cannot be wrong in saying that this person does not take the gift seriously. It is the same with a prophet who prophesies even when asleep. Is it proper for a gifted person to use the gift of God, which is intended to produce something good and divine for those for whom it is used, and at the same time lead a life which contradicts the goodness of God? The answer is 'no'. God intends the person who possesses the gift to realise the extent of God's love, and God's desire that His gift should be shared with others. 'For wisdom is a kindly spirit, yet she acquits not the blasphemer of his guilty lips; because God is the witness of his inmost self and the sure observer of his heart and the listener to his tongue. For the Spirit of the Lord fills the world, is all-embracing, and knows what man says' (Wisdom 1. 6–7).

It seems to me that we are like a little boy whose parents clothe him in Sunday-best to go to church. For a child even Sunday is a day on which he has to play, so he will throw himself down and play on the ground. He will spill food on the Sunday-best clothes (to him their value and their beauty do not mean much). By the end of the day the clothes need washing and mending. And how difficult it is for us to remain immaculate when called on by God to be at our best in life. We seem to be burned by the divine beauty with which we are clothed. How quickly we go back to our vomit, a life of play in the world, and when we return to God our Father we are so ugly as to be beyond recognition. God has made us in His Image, and has called us to be His own adopted children. In the matter at issue He still favours us in a very special way by endowing us with special gifts. But surrounded by all these favours we still do not appreciate God's generosity. 'We are truly his handiwork, created in Christ Jesus to lead the life of good deeds which God prepared for us in advance' (Ephesians 2.10). But do we allow ourselves to be treated as children who do not know the value of their clothes? Are you, like the child, more interested in a life which gives personal pleasure? How long do we have to be treated as children? Let me conclude with the following Scripture text: 'May you be filled with the knowledge of God's will through perfect wisdom and spiritual insight. Then you will lead a life worthy of the Lord and pleasing to him in every way. You will multiply good works of every sort and grow in the knowledge of God. By the might of his glory you will be endowed with the strength needed to stand fast, even to endure joyfully whatever may come, giving thanks to the Father for having made you worthy to share the lot of the saints in light. He rescued us from the power of darkness and brought us into the Kingdom of his beloved Son' (Colossians 1.9–13).

Prayer always

Setting time aside for prayer can not be considered 'time wasted', to the loss of other activities. If we believe in the advice of St Paul, 'Whatever you do, do it in the name of the Lord', we should consider *other* activities, done without being permeated by prayer, as 'time wasted'. If it is true that 'We should pray always', all human activity should have a divine balance. This means that the inflow of divine influence into human activity would colour the whole of it. Hence we would not hear of such distinctions as profane, secular, human or divine. The occupations of the individual who would 'pray always' must always be divine, because if would mean that the source and the driving force would be God, the Father of humanity and all that surrounds us. We came out of His hands and are answerable to Him in all we do. God is both the source of our life and our final destiny.

I have a special interest in stressing the words 'a divine balance'. We have often heard repeated in words and song that 'God is love'. This is true, and a person who loves God and is loved by Him should reflect the permanent character of God's love. To my surprise I have come across bitterness, irritability, impatience, authoritarianism, impure language and other vices which diminish the personality, in those who claim to represent God. If one only encounters it once, I think one can close one's eyes and ears to it. But when it becomes a set characteristic of a person, the Jesus that person claims to represent is certainly not the Jesus who laid down His life for those whom He loved to the last degree. If God is love, how can the people recognise Him as a loving Father in those who have 'specialised' in loving Him but who use authoritarian methods to convince them that they should be obedient children of God? If truly we priests have become little gods, it is incumbent on us to permeate all our activities with God's love. For me, prayer is the essential checking point of what we did yesterday and what we want to do, and what we have become used to doing.

My other reason for being interested in a 'divine balance' is my belief that Christianity represents the conquest of what is in us, but not its destruction. Through Christianity we learn to overcome our inclinations to evil, uproot the causes and in their place to cultivate virtues. Whatever gift we may have, without a 'divine balance' it is merely a show-off of power. For Jesus — who, if anyone, should show off power — is the merciful pastor, kind to the poor, the sick and all who need His help. As He approaches, the dawn of hope rises in them, and as He says to them 'Thy faith hath saved thee', they are completely overcome by His love and respect for them.

Prayer is essential to anyone who is engaged in the healing ministry. It is a process which reaches a climax at the time of actually offering special prayers for the sick. To walk into a room praying for the sick without calling the presence of God is a poor show of faith. It is like turning on a tap and drinking the water from unclean hands; there is no respect for the water, nor for the stomach that receives it dirty. It is not that the ministers are always dirty, but that we are in someone's field, and therefore it is wise and prudent to go together with Christ. We are using the power and authority of Christ, and that is why I prefer to see a minister engaged in the ministry of healing prepare himself for long enough before the actual offering of prayers for the sick.

How many privileged people have lost their gifts after some time? And how many have not even believed afterwards in what they had been doing? The interfering spirit has come in between and robbed them of their original divine gift. Yes, this is in the parable of the gardener who plants wheat, and finds cockle growing in the midst of the wheat the next time he visits his garden. Again we read in the parable of the sower that some seeds, having fallen on open ground, were picked up by the birds. Without prayer, gifted people slowly dry up spiritually. They increase their personal self-confidence outside Jesus. They lose their fear of the Lord. They act from routine and believe in the effectiveness of their methods. They become exhibitionists or even magicians, spiritual specialists. In the end, if they rely on themselves, they will tire and so withdraw from the field. It is good to know that a five-year-old boy cannot run against a fifteen-year-old, even if among his peers he is the best. He can only win if he is carried on the shoulder of the fifteen-year-old. Surely, the five-year-old will share the prize since they have done it together. So what? Yes, this is where we are. We won't win the race by ourselves. I have no intention of saying that our role is insignificant, but that what we are doing is so much above our ordinary understanding that we need to accept that we must lean on God's power, which we can continuously acquire through prayer.

I will bless the Lord at all times;
his praise shall continually be in my mouth.
My soul makes its boast in the Lord; let the afflicted hear and be glad.
O magnify the Lord with me, and let us exalt his name together!
I sought the Lord and he answered me, and delivered me from all my fears.
Look to him and be radiant; so your faces shall never be ashamed.
This poor man cried and the Lord heard him, and saved him from all his troubles.
The angel of the Lord encamps around those who fear him, and delivers them.
O taste and see that the Lord is good!
Happy is the man who takes refuge in him!
O fear the Lord, you his saints, for those who fear him have no want!
The young lions suffer want and hunger; but those who seek

the Lord lack for no good thing.
Come, O sons, listen to me, I will teach you the fear of the
Lord.   (Psalm 33. 1–11)

Contest with the powers of darkness

The health of the people at each end of the rope may determine
the victory in a tug-of-war. Added to the good health of each
team must be the knowledge of the game. It is not so much the
weight of each member which will determine the victory, but
rather how, together with the others, that weight is put into one
common act. In the tug-of-war the whole team must feel heavy
together, just as much as they must pull together. If victory is to
be considered a possibility, it is important to peep into the
strength of the other team: one must know who they are and how
often they have played the game, and then look at their
apparent strength, how robust they seem to be. Appearances
have often led human judgement astray.

We are engaged in a tug-of-war with the powers of darkness,
and are for ever pulling people between them and ourselves. We
are assured of the victory, but we need to know how to go about
it. You have just read about standing firm against the evil spirits.
I am now going to tell you what you should do when you are
actually conversing with the evil one. You are aiming at winning
back the victim of possession, and thus restoring the victim's self-
mastery. This is where the tug-of-war begins.

In the realm of exorcism, the advice which we receive from
those engaged in the ministry of deliverance is that we must
identify the enemy by name. The enemy may be put into a con-
vulsion or a trance, and tortured in many ways, but as long as he
is not identified he can believe that the prayers are not directed
to him. Hence it is good to ask the following questions:

1. Who are you?
2. How many are you?
3. How long have you been with him/her?
4. Where is your habitation in him/her?
5. What disease have you caused in him/her?

Do not worry much about the order of the questions. What I
have found most important is to find out immediately who they
are and how many they are. The other questions can come in any

order. It is not always easy to get the answers as one likes, and at a time of one's choosing. Again out of the answers one must watch for some which must be taken with a pinch of salt; they are not always straightforward. After some experience one comes to know what should be taken seriously and what put aside as lies. The devil and his company are not at all shocked when you call them liars. They usually say, 'Oh! so you know us.'

Here again one must not tire of repeatedly using the authority of Jesus. When the spirits are dumb, which often means only that they do not want to speak, one must certainly use the authority of Jesus: 'I order you in the name of Jesus to tell me the truth: who are you? I order you in the name of Jesus to speak and to tell me your names.' At certain moments they may only move the tongue and whisper some words. One must go on insisting that the devil will speak distinctly. (As we have already said, while using the authority of Jesus, one must have the necessary disposition truly to represent Him.) The answers from the evil one and his company are not pleasing to hear. If at this stage one reacts as if one would kick the evil spirits if one were to see them, then it is wise to cut short the questioning and go directly to the function of exorcism. I repeat again: *never* get angry with the evil spirits; use the authority of Jesus and be inwardly calm and confident. An agitated person may be a quick thinker, but the value of the things one thinks of and utters in this condition is questionable. A calm, slow, ponderous person may say fewer words in a minute than a quick thinker, but it may be that each word has three times the value of the many words of the quick thinker. The higher the tone of voice of the exorcist, the more he needs to reflect deeply on what he is saying. If it only means stressing a point to the evil spirits, then the value of what he says is not so much in the tone, but in the meaning of the words he utters. He must win the tug-of-war, but he needs to root himself in Jesus Christ.

There are some exorcists who use the Church ritual. There are others who use the prayers approved by Pope Leo XIII, part of which were said after Mass in the old Latin rite. I appreciate in both the direct exorcism against the evil one and his company. There is no beating about the bush; in these rituals the devil is called by his name 'Satan'. Undoubtedly no exorcist will omit personal and spontaneous prayers. These are important. When one is in sorrow one often utters words and expressions which have very deep meaning. When the exorcist reaches a stage where he feels he has exhausted the prayers in the ritual, or that more meaningful words should be added to the fixed prayers, let him go ahead and say what the Lord tells him to say. It is appropriate and right to do so. Exorcists find themselves in very different situations and circumstances, and by saying some prayers as the situation seems to demand and not being satisfied with what they have recited in the ritual, they merely show that they understand the importance of a personal share and involvement in what they are doing.

On the other hand, the exorcist must know that there are no special prayers for expelling the different ranks of the evil spirits. At the moment when he meets them in this tug-of-war, they say what they feel they should say, regardless of what the exorcist says in his prayers. It is important therefore to know how to say spontaneous prayers so as to prepare oneself for any eventuality. The hundred and one evil spirits may be expelled from a person as the exorcist reaches the end of the recitation of the prayers in the ritual. But in exorcising a person possessed by Satan himself ('the great dragon' [Rev.12.9]), a lot more is needed than mere recitation of the fixed prayers for exorcism. Satan can stand the mention of the name 'Jesus', and can also repeat it several times, although it pinches him. He is able to hold a very sound conversation with the exorcist, remaining logical and calm. He can demonstrate his power and physically torture the victim before the exorcist. Those who are not aware of his tactics are thrown off balance by this manifestation of his personality. As he does this, the exorcist should concentrate on some proper words to answer. Often on these occasions I have referred to Scriptures, and have always found a proper word with which to answer him.

My dear brothers and sisters, the tug-of-war is something we must win. Our captain Jesus Christ beat Satan and his company on the Cross, accepting the challenge of this last attempt used by the devil, namely death. He was flashed out of life, but he rose from it victoriously, with a splendour and power far beyond that of Satan. As He once more walked on this globe, His enemies were unable to face Him again on the same footing. He pulled them away in the tug-of-war, and they all fell at His feet, and were left afraid, mesmerised and defeated. Jesus has done it for us. It is up to us now to walk the same path that Jesus walked, and with Him put the evil one and his company to shame. 'And Jesus came and said to them: "All authority in heaven and on earth has been given to me. Go therefore and make disciples of all nations, baptising them in the name of the Father and of the Son and of the Holy Spirit, teaching them to observe all that I have commanded you; and lo, I am with you always, to the close of the age" ' (Matthew 28.18−20).

Let us have confidence in Him. He is with us always. He has authority in heaven and on earth to do whatever He wants with creation. He wants humanity to be completely free from the bondage of Satan. Hence He has full authority over Satan and all his powers. Jesus overcame him at all points. Let us believe that this is the way to win the tug-of-war.

We must have confidence in God, and never lose sight of Him in all we do. Our connecting chain with Him is prayer. Then follows intimacy with Him. What we call faith is a replica of God's life in us. We have exchanged rights with God, and we can trust that when we say 'In God's name let this be done', then it will be done because we know that He will not disappoint us. His permanent presence in us, in other words, means that we move in Him, and are possessed by Him. We should rather use the term 'are living in Him', as St John says: 'We can be sure that we are in God only when the one who claims to be living in Him is living the same kind of life as Christ lived' (I John 2.5−6).

This is the one necessary condition for doing the things Christ did, and being able to use His name and authority. The life of Jesus in us is not easily acquired. We must be ready to walk with Him in the path to Gethsemane and not shrink at the sight of trials before us. For us as sinners this is a purifying process, nibbling away at the roots of sin in us till we break with it. St John says: 'Surely everyone who entertains this hope must purify himself, must try to be as pure as Christ. Anyone who sins at all breaks the law, because to sin is to break the law. Now you know that He appeared in order to abolish sin, and that in Him there is no sin; anyone who lives in God does not sin and anyone who sins has never seen Him, or known Him' (John 3.3−6).

Our role in the healing ministry is a humble one, not just because we must be humble, but rather because the effects of what we do are beyond what we are usually able to do as human beings. To level a mountain usually takes strong machines and a lot of money. But if we believe in God we can move a mountain in less than a minute. As we finish uttering the words, the mountain is moved. Certainly it is beyond our human capabilities, hence our need for humility. Let us be humble then before God, and be fair to ourselves and to God Himself. We give Him His due honour and praise.

(*Precautions in the Ministry of Deliverance*, pp. 13–20, 28–37)

3

AFRICAN SPIRITUALITY

[Milingo claims on the one hand that what he does in the ministry of healing and deliverance is in no way peculiar to Africa, and he can point to numerous examples from Europe and America to prove this. On the other hand, he maintains that there is an African view of religion, an African spirituality, which has been ignored and overlaid by Western rationality, and that this ignorance and contempt for African thought is a cause of spiritual tension. In *The Demarcations* he speaks strongly of the Western attitude; sometimes expressed even through missionaries:]

The healing ministry has been a façade to point at for many missionaries. The crux of the matter lies in the struggle to remain who they are, without change. They have enjoyed the privilege of piloting evangelisation, they cannot accept being piloted. They have never accepted mashawe as a disease worth healing, since they call it by their own name as a hysterical and psychosomatic disease, and they therefore consider anyone engaged in fighting it as an imbecile who chases the wind.

(*Demarcations*, p. 128)

In the field of liturgy, we have been surprised that those who have specialised in African liturgical adaptations are the Westerners. They have come to teach Africans accepted gestures, movements and drums. What they approve, we Africans must approve. What they do not like, we must give up. They have gone so far as to incite the Africans themselves to condemn their own traditional values supposed to be included in the liturgy. The principle to guide them is that there is nothing pure and sacred in all that is African; they pose before us as the sacred and pure, having the spirit of discernment for genuine African values worthy to be included in the liturgy. Our Africanness is with us and in us. We have been fed on it and so brought up in it. They tell me that I have no discipline since I do not send away from the church all the ladies with crying

babies during my sermon. During baptism I must tell all the
mothers to hide their breasts when they bring their babies. 'Tell
them to breast-feed their babies before baptism. . . .' As I wait
for the people to come in before Mass I am told, 'This is not good
education. When will the people learn to be on time?' As we
come together to pray I am told, 'Will you teach them to sing
quietly? Singing is also prayer, why do they have to shout? More-
over they are singing at every moment which is left free. They
should learn to have some silent moments. . . .'

(*Demarcations*, pp. 134–5)

Very little has been known of African music. In Africa composers of music are found in every field. They make it naturally.
We have music for pounding maize. We have music for evening
recreation in the moonlight. We have funeral music, initiation
music and marriage music. The composers of this music do not
claim rights over it, and it becomes a community property. We
have lived with this music. Some of it is accompanied by musical
instruments, and as the melody beats up, the voices and the
musical instruments go up too. So I am told: 'They have no self-
control. They should not be controlled by drums, rather they
should control the drums. In the end we do not hear the words of
the hymn, the drums drown all the words.' This is how we are
being civilised. Our traditions must be reshaped to suit the
Western mind before they can be accepted as worth preserving.
They advise me that it is my duty to co-operate with them to edu-
cate my fellow-Africans. They accept the importance of the fact
that I am an African, but they value me much more as the
instrument to bring a change to African attitudes and culture
according to their wishes. They are shaping me as one shapes an
ordinary blunt blade into a slasher. (*Demarcations*, pp. 135–6)

How patient Africa is, she has been patient from the day my own
ancestors stepped on her till now. My own mother grew up in her
African tradition and she never had an ambition to be a
European. Neither did she feel that by leading an African life
she missed something. To convince me that I can only be a full
Christian when I shall be well brought up in European civilisation and culture is to force me to change my nature. If God made
a mistake by creating me an African it is not yet evident. My
antagonists have not yet given me summons to call me to the

High Court of God where he will undo me as an African in order
to make me a European as a *conditio sine qua non* for becoming
a full Christian. (*Demarcations*, p. 11)

[Milingo frequently speaks of African awareness of a spirit world,
which he names 'the world-in-between', a world between this one and
'the final world where God the Father and Creator is' (*Healing*, p. 20).
Above the spirit world there is God the Father:]

God is Father because he protects his children and is accessible
to them. He is their security and supplier of all human needs.
This is the God whom we need in Africa. A God who is a real
father, one who cares for his children, protects them, gives them
security and is accessible. The God who is said to be in the Holy
Heaven, who is at peace with himself and does not care about
what is happening among the people on earth, is certainly not an
African God. This distant God is the one whom the Africans
miss in their churches on Sunday. He is far from them. He is a
special God who remains in the Church as preached by Western
Christianity. The African traditional God is the One who walks
with them, and whom they consult any time a need arises. It is
the God who lives with them. (*Demarcations*, p. 142)

There is no doubt at all that God is the one who deserved the
name 'father'. However, in many African traditions all the
attributes of a mother are also given to God. Therefore God is
both male and female, father and mother. He is the one who
brings into being — 'the highest creator'. The concept of fer-
tility is attributed to women, so since God brings into being all
creation including human beings, He therefore is a mother. For
this reason in traditional prayers a woman expresses herself
freely as a woman, and knows that she will be understood
without any need for explanation. A man too has a right to pray
in his own way as a man. Is it not from a woman that one is born
female? Is it not from the same woman that one is born male?
This double potency is transmitted from God, the highest creator. He shares it with men and women. I have never heard my
mother giving God a gender. I have asked a Malawian whether
his language has a gender for God. He gave several names of
God, and none had a gender; the names explained or defined
the actions of God. God is father because he sustains life. In my
African tradition He is father because He is the principle of life,

and gives growth to it. He is the source of life. 'If one has a father, one has a direction in life,' so it is said.

(*Demarcations*, p. 141)

The attachment to the ancestral worship among Africans combines the respect for the dead who are now near the Great One, and the power they have after death over earthly problems. They have control over a lot of earthly elements, and at the same time they are now able to fight the evil spirits which send evil spells on the living. I have heard of a Lenje prayer to the ancestors, which runs as follows: 'You our ancestors who were so good while you were with us. You were kind to us. Help us to have rain. Speak to the High One, the Great Spirit, to send us rain.'

(*Black Civilisation and the Catholic Church*, 1977, p. 11)

Knowledge of the unknown

The Africans have been communing with their dead ancestors from time beyond reckoning. It is the one thing which colonisation never succeeded in suppressing. The Church believed that since whatever they said was accepted, so all the Christians stopped communing with their dead ancestors. But if the Church had been wise, it would have penetrated the funeral rituals, marriage ceremonies, naming rituals, and so on. These are the areas where the Africans have still remained themselves, and thanks be to God that this has happened because otherwise we should have no identity. Many of the so-called educated are ignorant in these matters. We are what we are because our society still has something special; we can speak with the dead, and a community may thus be guided in its endeavour to carry out decisions which affect the whole community.

There have always remained prophets among us who have foretold coming events and the calamities that threaten the community. They have given warning in due time, and so people have been able to prepare themselves to face the coming danger. Since all these things were considered superstitious, they have only continued to happen in the community under cover for fear of offending the messengers of the Good News. There are now more than 4,000 African independent churches in South Africa, rebelling against the imported Good News, which they feel has not proved good enough for the Africans. In Nigeria there are also many independent churches, which have cast off the bond of Western religious determinism in the approach to preaching the Good News to the Africans. What a ready field the continent of Africa was for spiritual cultivation and planting, but the Church came to us in human form and with human means. I do not remember so far in the archdiocese of Lusaka any parish priest who was so trusted by his parishioners that they were open with him and came to him with their real problems. The hesitant way of giving answers to problems, and the postponement of final decisions still to come from final consultations, put off many troubled souls, while the clients of Mr X. and Mrs Y. get their answers easily, as they can consult them at any time. Is it strange, then, that the people tend to believe that one can ask a priest only what he knows from his academic and theological studies, and nothing beyond? The traditional spiritual consultant speaks to the ancestors and other protective spirits and they give the answer. Yes, they often mislead the people, but does the Church offer alternatives and preach the absolute when the Christians need answers to their problems?

Only when we shall present God not as an élite figure but as a Father to the Africans, one who can be turned to on occasions such as those enumerated above, only then will He be an African God. It is not surprising that while the people go to church on Sunday they have an attitude of praying for what they call 'decent' problems, fit to be presented to a God who belongs to the upper class. He is so high that He has no time for the petty problems of an African who hardly knows the proper language to use as he speaks to Him, and who thinks he will never have a chance to hear His voice. As a Kenyan nun said to me, 'We leave him in the church on Sunday and ask our ancestral gods to accompany us for the rest of the week.' She went on to say, speaking of retreats: 'They oblige us to keep silent for eight days. Does it take so long to speak to God?'

When God is presented to us in simple terms as one who is truly concerned with our daily problems, we will accept him. Then the Church will win Africa faster than it has done up till now.   (*Plunging into Darkness*, pp. 15–17)

[Milingo finds in the person of Jesus the link through which this African spirituality can be transformed into a Christian spirituality. Jesus fills for all humanity the role of a supreme ancestor.]

Jesus the Ancestor

Giving Jesus the title of Ancestor is not just giving Him an honorary title. Jesus fits perfectly into the African understanding of ancestor. He is more than that, but we can find in Him all that we Africans are looking for in our ancestors. This is a very noble title, because when we consider Jesus as an ancestor, it means that he is to us an elder in the community, an intercessor between God (Mwari, the high god) and our community, and the possessor of ethereal powers which enable Him to commune with the world above and with the earth. He is able to be a citizen of both worlds. This is the availability of Jesus.

Until the people see the role of Jesus as being in the hierarchy of the spirit-world, that is of our ancestors, it will be hard to uproot them completely from their beliefs. Jesus deserves the complete commitment to Him of the human race; He is truly the elder of the human family, 'the first-born of them all'. The following Bible text should make my fellow-Africans consider seriously the role of Jesus in the hierarchy of the spirit world: 'For this reason, because I have heard of your faith in the Lord Jesus and your love towards all the saints, I do not cease to give thanks for you, remembering you in my prayers, that the God of our Lord Jesus Christ, the Father of Glory, may give you a Spirit of Wisdom and of revelation in the knowledge of him, having the eyes of your hearts enlightened, that you may know what is the hope to which he has called you, what are the riches of his glorious inheritance in the saints, and what is the immeasurable greatness of His power in us who believe . . . And he has put all things under His feet and has made Him the *head* over all things for the Church, which is His body, the fulness of Him who fills all in all' (Ephesians 1. 15–23).

When Paul was speaking to the Jews and Greeks, he had to take into consideration the fact that they had their own beliefs. Among the Jews the coming of Jesus had been looked forward to, but they had their own concept of what He, as their Messiah, was going to do for them. When Paul speaks to the Jews and Gentiles he accepts that he too is what he is, after his conversion, only by the grace of God. He confesses that he himself was subject to wrong beliefs, and thus was a sinner. As he preached to them he confessed his sins, enumerating the vices which had controlled him. In this way he was able to help both Jews and Greeks to have a good disposition to listen to him and to accept Jesus Christ and His message: 'And you he made alive, when you were dead through the trespasses and sins in which you once walked, following the course of this world, following the prince of the power of the air, the spirit that is now at work in the sons of disobedience. Among these we all once lived in the passions of our flesh following the desires of body and mind, and so were by nature children of wrath, like the rest of mankind' (Ephesians 2. 2–4).

It is no longer a kindness to say of the Africans, 'They are naturally religious', when our attitude as we preach to them is that of giving them a 'new god', one they do not know. The attitude of anger, sometimes called 'zeal for the glory of God', which is a false justification for a spiritual superiority complex, has to be wiped away from within us. We must plead with our people and ask them for a hearing. The roots of their beliefs in the power of the spirit-world are not just a social accommodation in their community, but are convictions that their ancestors give them guidance to plan their destinies.

Is it true that the modern African Church has failed to produce a saint from ordinary life? And if it is true, is it a small matter? If there are saints, what form has their sainthood taken and who is going to proclaim them as saints? That will depend on how Africans will accept Jesus and His message and relate it to their own way of life. There is no doubt at all that Jesus is an elder, not only by being the 'first-born', but also by the fact that He took over the responsibility of an elder after rising from the dead. Our ancestors take up this rank after they have died. They are expected to take on the guardianship of the clan, the tribe, the community, and to be much more enlightened about the affairs of the community than they were when still alive on earth. Jesus deserves to be an elder, not just because He died and rose from the dead, but also because he beat all his enemies — death, sin and Satan. He is an elder in the sense that He is greater than all His enemies. He is an all-powerful elder, and we are clearly right to seek protection from one who is all-powerful.

Jesus the Intercessor

It was a painstaking effort on the part of Paul to replace Moses, Melchisedek and the priestly rank by Jesus in the Jewish community. We have no right to blame the Jews for their stubbornness. They had lived in the same way for hundreds of years. Moses was to them a great hero and liberator. Melchisedek was their mysterious figure, who came into their midst in a strange way; they could not trace his ancestral origins. They were happy that he was one of them, offering sacrifices on their behalf. And so immediately Paul puts Jesus in relation with Melchisedek: 'We have this as a sure and steadfast anchor of the soul, a hope that enters into the inner shrine behind the curtain, where Jesus has gone as a forerunner on our behalf, having become a high priest for ever after the order of Melchisedek' (Hebrews 6. 19–20).

Look at the analysis of what the Jews drew from the presence of Melchisedek: 'For this Melchisedek, King of Salem, Priest of the Most High God, met Abraham returning from the slaughter of the Kings and blessed him, and to him Abraham apportioned a tenth part of everything. He is first, by translation of his name, King of Righteousness, and he is also King of Salem, that is, King of Peace. He is without father or mother or genealogy, and has neither beginning of days nor end of life, but resembling the Son of God he continues a priest forever' (Hebrews 7. 1–3). This is how the Jews were able to see the role of Jesus in relation to the high priest.

Still, Paul felt that it was necessary to prove that Jesus was more than a high priest, and a higher priest than Melchisedek: 'Those who formerly became priests took their office without an oath, but this one was addressed with an oath, "The Lord has sworn and will not change his mind, thou art a priest forever." This makes Jesus the surety of a better covenant' (Hebrews 7. 21). As for Moses, here is how Paul puts it to the Jews: 'For when every commandment of the law had been declared by Moses to all the people, he took the blood of calves and goats, with water and scarlet wool and hyssop, and sprinkled both the book itself and all the people, saying, "This is the blood of the covenant which God commanded you" ' (Hebrews 9. 19–20).

When one observes Paul speaking to the Jews, the necessity of understanding people's approach to God becomes clear. Christianity, as we have seen already, is a conqueror but not a destroyer of what exists. It uplifts beliefs, purifies them and adds something better. Comparing the role of Moses to that of Jesus, Paul says to the Jews: 'For if the sprinkling of defiled persons with the blood of goats and bulls and with the ashes of a heifer sanctifies for the purification of the flesh, how much more shall the blood of Christ, who through the eternal spirit offered himself without blemish to God, purify your conscience from the dead works to serve the living God. Therefore he is the mediator of a new covenant, so that those who are called may receive the promised eternal inheritance, since a death has occured which redeems them from the transgressions under the first covenant' (Hebrews 9. 13–15).

It is painful to realise that for many people Jesus is still only vaguely understood as living, and hence as a person who is continuously interceding for us before the Father. We have often failed to portray Him as a living person because we have not learned the ways by which our people commune with their ancestral mediators. Their methods look to us funny and of low spiritual worth. 'They are not even worth studying,' we say. We have preached Christ, and have failed to put Him into the lives of our people, despite the fact that He is God-*man*. The concept that since He died He has been watching every wayward child who neglects to take the means of redemption, has deprived us of our most important gift, the gift of freedom. Just as Paul knew that the Jews had only one great priest, one great mediator and one great sacrifice, he still approached them, in order that they should accept Jesus, with respect and a sense of seeking their approval. They had first to understand and accept what was presented to them as a richer spiritual harvest than what they were used to. They had to be shown the truth of what was now being promised. And Paul was lucky to live at the time of the triumph of the resurrection, which was followed by many divine signs and miracles. Paul lived to reflect the life of Jesus and the power of His message.

It makes me sad that we preachers of Christ's message today feel that it is to our advantage if the power of intercession of our ancestors has proved unreliable. It is possible that the clients of today do not perform the full prescribed ritual when they pray to the ancestors. They too are modern unbelievers. I have come across many sick people who have been at several traditional consultations without success. I know a family who just could not stick to their gods when they noticed that their problems were not solved in spite of the daily family ritual in their homes. In their anger they smashed the effigies which represented the Nshila gods in their families. What saddens me even more is the fact that they came to us at the last moment. Why had they not realised before that Jesus was their greatest intercessor? I am thinking of a couple who are Catholic, well married in church, but in spite of their Christian background they brought into their family the Nshila effigies for protection and guardianship. Only when these gods failed to bring peace in the family did they come to us. The wife had stayed away from her husband for six months under the care of the traditional spiritual consultant, the medium between her and the guardian spirits.

Was it necessary to prove the guardian spirits ineffective first before we could offer them the greater power of Jesus? This question has troubled me deeply. St Paul did not say to the Jews that the blood of goats and bulls was ineffective. He only pointed out that the Blood of Christ has much greater efficacy. If our people can turn with their problems to the ancestral spirits, must we go and smash their effigies to make them turn to the great, true and living ancestor, Jesus Christ? Anyway, we offered this family the protection of Jesus. Today they are happy together as a united family, without spirit interference. The Nshila gods are gone and their importance has vanished too. Yes, we are living in the era of Jesus. He has replaced the ancient gods and their priests. He has neutralised their power, unless they work with him. None of the gods, not even those of my clan, can make themselves the end of any people's worship. All now must channel their worship to God through Jesus Christ. Let us prove it by confidently calling on Jesus as we introduce the people to Him.

I was consoled to read a conversation between Ndabaningi Sithole and Mutezo in the former's book *Obed Mutezo of Zimbabwe*. I found in it something which led me to a realisation of how scrupulous I should be when presenting the Gospel to my fellow-Africans. That they have their own way of incorporating

Jesus into their beliefs became clear as one reflects upon the answers of Mutezo.

Ndabaningi Sithole: 'Since you believe in *midzimu* [spirits, plural] and now you believe in Christianity, doesn't this cause confusion in your mind or heart?'

Mutezo: 'There is no confusion. *Midzimu* means that those who are said to be dead are not really dead. They are alive. They are in the keeping of Mwari, or God, Himself. Christianity teaches that there is eternal life. There is immortality. People don't really die and disappear but their souls go to heaven. They live forever, just as in *midzimu* worship and my Christian beliefs.'

Sithole: 'Do you remember the words of Jesus, "No one comes to the Father but through me"? In *midzimu* worship we approach God through our immediate and remote ancestors, not through Jesus Christ.'

Mutezo: 'I take it that Jesus had become the ancestor for everybody. In other words he is now a *mudzimu* [spirit, singular] for everybody, whereas my *midzimu* are only for the Mutezo family. I do not see anything wrong in approaching God through the *mudzimu* for everybody or through the Mutezo *mudzimu*.'

It is fortunate that Mutezo was able to express himself so freely in this conversation. I can imagine how hard it would be for me to ask these questions objectively without feeling within me an urge to give an immediate instruction. 'He has been leading a false Christian life,' I would think, and then I would go into qualms of conscience as to how he came to water down the Christian message to such a low level as to make Christian beliefs start from traditional beliefs. Mutezo takes the resurrection of the dead from his own understanding of the immortality of the *midzimu*. He compares Jesus as an intercessor with his own Mutezo clan spirit. He accepts that Jesus is a universal intercessor who does not suppress the Mutezo spirit. He says there is nothing wrong in it.

Can an African be a Christian?

It shocked a Ugandan scholar, Phares Mutibwa, to reflect upon an African's approach to Christianity and he asked himself,

'Can an African really be a Christian?' I dare answer immediately with a big 'YES'. But he cannot make it if he is asked to
be, for example, a Belgian, German, Swedish, English or Canadian Christian, or any other kind of 'national' Christian. It is
easy for 'Christianity to become somebody', but not for somebody to become a Christian in the form and culture of a nation
other than his/her own. Christianity can be Belgian, German,
English, French, and so on, but the spirit of Christianity, the
Spirit of Christ, cannot be appropriated by any nation. That is
why Jesus is a universal Saviour and I as an African am entitled
to draw from Him all that I need as an African, and He will
build me up without reserve, regardless of what He does to the
Belgians, French, English and the rest of them. When we all
meet, full of the gifts of Jesus, we shall appreciate all the more
the fairness of Jesus as He deals with every nation according to its
needs. A fair deal is needed with African traditional beliefs:
'The dialogue between Christianity and African religions, which
is now going on, is a most welcome one; but it should be used in
order to arrive at a much clearer understanding of why we
believe in what we believe rather than as a mere rejection of one
religion and its replacement by another' (Mutibwa, *African
Heritage and the New Africa,* 1977).

How hard it will be to make myself believe that my father is
not Cilola, when I know that I carry his blood in my veins, and
has been replaced by a noble person called Chinde.* I have first
to go back to find out in what ways Chinde compares with my
father Cilola, and whether he compares favourably. I may not
be prepared to accept the advantage which I am going to receive
from Chinde, as I am attached to my father, who helped me
through all my difficult times. Being 'chindelised' may be a
painless process, but it does not touch my real being which I
share with my father Cilola, who is the backbone and core of my
being. Is it fair to him that I should cut myself off from him for
an 'advantage' that seems to me no greater than a dish of
potatoes? The only way to 'chindelise' me properly is to carry my
father Cilola with me. Make an African a Christian *with* his

[* Cilola is a clan name which in this text represents African traditional religion; Chinde represents a foreign religion, i.e. Christianity.]

beliefs in ancestral spirits and, just as Paul showed the Jews the superiority of Jesus over Moses, Melchisedek and the Jewish sacrifice of the blood of bulls and goats, so should the Africans be reasoned with too, because the respect they have for their ancestors is a noble quality.

Ndabaningi Sithole says of Mutezo that he 'was not a clean slate or blank sheet in which the missionaries, the evangelists, the preachers and the Christian teachers wrote their Christian beliefs and practices. He accepted Christianity in the light of his own concrete experience and still interprets it in that light, and this has been the history of Christianity since the first century.' What Ndabaningi Sithole says here has been said many times, but still one notices with what negligence the Gospel is preached. It speaks of abstract things, which often have no relevance to man's day-to-day activities. What is preached is *about Jesus*, not so much *Jesus Himself*. We should teach people to speak of Jesus as we speak of a living person. They should learn to address Him as simply as they address any one of their friends, except that they do not see Him, even 'Jesus, please take care of my baby as I am going to the market. Please see to it that nothing harmful happens to her.' (It would be quite natural for an African mother to invoke such protection, even if she is leaving another member of the family at home with the baby.) It is a simple, direct relationship.

Taking the Africans with their beliefs into Christianity is a necessary step on the way to their full conversion. I am not giving approval to all the gods of the Africans, but rather saying that in the long run, by elimination, they will be locked up in their '*kacises*', or family shrines. What I do not approve of is the condemnatory attitude, which has now left us so ignorant of the power of Africans' beliefs that we cannot properly understand why they have not left their old gods when we are certain that we can offer them everything in Jesus Christ. Why has Jesus not permeated their whole lives after Baptism and Confirmation? This is a serious question. They say that Pdma Sambhava, founder of Tibetan Buddhism, did it well. He even succeeded in taming a thousand local demons and changing them into the guardians of the faith of the people of the Himalayas. One is free to accept the story with a pinch of salt, but it proved to his followers that the

Buddha had power over the demons who reigned in the Himalayas.

It is due to my personal anguish that I have decided to share my experience with my fellow-ministers. When on 10 January 1978 I stopped dealing with people's problems every Tuesday and Friday, I was dealing with 500 people a week. Many of them had passed through the hands of several traditional healers and spiritual consultants. Some of their problems could have been dealt with by priests in the different parishes; however, even if I had sent them to the priests as I was ordered to do, I do not believe that they would have gone — the reason being that they presumed that they would not be understood, or that the priests do not deal with such intimate personal problems. On the other hand, one is shocked to hear the qualifications of those to whom they submit themselves, and to whom they so easily open their hearts; they do so because they accept the traditional healers and spiritual consultants as a class of people endowed with mysterious power. The missionary priests laugh at such assumptions or attribute their powers to devils, just as in Europe every liberation movement in Africa is believed to be Communist.

These quick ready-made answers to every African problem have destroyed the seed of mutual trust between African traditional religions and Western Christianity. We cannot go on hiding God as we are doing. (By 'we' I mean ministers of the Christian religion.) We are protecting God from being spoilt by African traditional religion, and we cannot pinpoint which elements of the latter are evil. A vast number of our Christians are ancestral worshippers, and proud of it. I could cite endless examples — like a well-known, well-to-do woman who, by order of her ancestral spirits, has remained single. The spirit-elders ordered her: 'You know that I was a chief. Remember once a year to kill a cow in my honour. I want the people to celebrate in my name. You are married to our clan and to nobody else.' The words are from her dead ancestor. She is a graduate of a famous Catholic school, a Christian in and out. So it is beyond my understanding how we can go on shifting away from African traditional religion if we truly want to see the Africans become Christians with their whole selves. I do not want to share in this culpable ignorance and escapism.

The existence of Peter Kiari's writings in defence of African traditional religions make me feels a little less like a 'voice in the wilderness'. Peter considers it a necessity to study them seriously, and to see them in their own African colours and values: 'What the African people need is not "Christianity" meaning "concrete historical expressions of Christianity as lived and developed in different parts of the world". What the African people need is Jesus Christ preached to them, and him crucified, dead, buried and risen from the dead — the Good News.' He goes on: 'The concrete expression of Africa's response to Jesus Christ preached to them will have to be determined by the values and insights of the Traditional African Religious Heritage. This requirement I do not consider to be an optional extra, but rather as necessary if the message of Jesus Christ is going to take root among African peoples. The alternative will be having "flowerpot" Christianity whose survival and vitality depends on continued watering by missionaries' (Peter P. Kiari Njooroge, *Practical Ecumenism*).

The answer is Jesus, and I am certain that the Africans will themselves do the sifting of their religious values when they come across the power of Jesus Christ. It will not be strange to them to carry Jesus in place of their living-dead ancestors by whom they are used to being possessed. The living-dead ancestors are cultured and well-mannered people. They will give way when Jesus comes in, provided that Jesus guarantees protection and guardianship to the living members of the clans and tribes. He will undoubtedly do so with pleasure, since we know that He has spent Himself completely for the restoration of man's dignity and for his redemption: 'And they sang a new song, saying, "worthy art thou to take the scroll and to open its seals, for thou wast slain and by thy blood didst ransom men for God from every tribe and tongue and people and nation, and hast made them a kingdom and priests to our God, and they shall reign on earth" ' (Rev. 5. 9–10).

The availability of Jesus

We are marrying Jesus with our ancestors. Some of my readers may be inclined to think that I am merely making a comparison between the two, and leave it at that. But Jesus has all that our ancestors have and more. I have only to prove it, and so convince my people that they should put their full confidence in Jesus. I have no objection if at the same time they will carry along their ancestors, who will contribute to their welfare together with Jesus. I cannot imagine that my grandmothers and grandfathers are in hell. If the redemption brought by Jesus was effective for Isaac, Abraham and Lot, should it not be effective for my ancestors? Certainly, they too were somehow included in anticipation in the redemption wrought for the whole human race by Jesus Christ. They must be envious that I was born late enough to have the privilege of being a priest. If any of them were still in purgatory, I am certain they are out now, since I pray for the souls in purgatory every Monday. I pray for my dead parents and relatives every Friday. So my grandparents may rest in peace and be given an eternal reward.

Marrying Jesus with our ancestors means carrying over the trust our people have in their ancestors into Jesus. They will believe in Jesus and trust Him when they feel close to Him and *experience* that He is alive among them just as their ancestors are. That is why we have to define the ethereal powers possessed by our ancestors which we know Jesus Christ possesses too. The ethereal powers here mean that our ancestors, after death, are no longer restricted when traversing this earth by being subject to the laws of gravity, distance or time; they do not have the burden of carrying a body, since they are now spirits. They are able to be with the living at any time that they are called upon, or when they decide to commune with the living. Our people believe too that after death the ancestors acquire new power which they did not have when they were alive. Some are feared, which is why the living often observe the advice from the dead scrupulously. But when they come as peaceful spirits, they look forward to hearing them from time to time. Hence they like to consult them on many occasions.

Is it really the dead who come and speak to the living? For me this is beyond discussion, because I have dealt with many of them. Let me just give one example. One day a woman came to my office and called me to follow her to the hospital where her sister was very sick. We went together to the hospital, and when we arrived we found that the sister was dead. I went into the room and took hold of her hand. I was able to ascertain what had killed her, but the cries of people were such that I could scarcely utter an audible word of prayer. Realising that there was nothing more I could do for her I was able to give her absolution because she was still warm.

Then came the day for the funeral Mass. During the Mass, at the time of the consecration, I felt a sudden force pulling me towards the corpse. I placed myself straight in front of it and went on praying intensely for the departed spirit. After the funeral one of her sisters could not overcome her sorrow, and they brought her to me. I took her into my private chapel and we began to talk. It was not long before I found myself talking with her dead sister who had just been buried. She smiled and said to me: 'Thank you for arriving in time at my bedside and for giving me absolution. I was going to be condemned and now that you have offered Mass for me, I am happy with God.' I excused myself for having arrived late at her bedside in the hospital, and said that I could not do more than just give her absolution. She answered: 'It was decided that I should die. But you know what happened. . . .' Then she explained the cause of her death. She was speaking through this sister of hers, because she loved her especially and she knew that she was the one who would suffer most from her death. Even now, if we want to have messages from her, we can use the sister as a medium. The dead sister has often come to her.

On another occasion I struggled with the devil and his company in a woman. He confessed to me: 'There were two of your people with us, Malama and Mwape. They are now gone.' The devil said they were gone, but we knew that this was not true. They came to our side and were fighting the devil with us, and even if the woman had suffered for many years, they had still prevented much evil which could have befallen her if they had not been there. These protecting spirits are very gentle and reasonable, and obedient to our orders. On yet another occasion, out of thirty spirits presumed to be evil, I was surprised to find that ten were guardian spirits. They said to me: 'We are glad that you have sent away the evil spirits. It took us a long time to bring the patient here. We are happy that we have achieved our aim.' They wanted to hold a long conversation with me, but I always feel an obligation not to abuse a patient by using him/her as a means of information; it is not right for me to forget my strict duty to deliver the possessed from the evil spirits, and begin taking interest in what the spirits say. If there is something important in connection with 'healing' or 'deliverance', I know that He in whose name I work will let me know. However, on this occasion I thanked them and they were very glad. I said to them: 'May I know your names?' The names they gave me were very rare and strange. I went on to ask: 'How do I contact you? Can I rely on your help?' They answered: 'Yes, count on us.' They were very gentle and obedient to me, and answered every question briefly and courteously. The tone of authority which I had when I spoke to the evil spirits was changed: I was obliged to be also soft and relaxed.

It will certainly be more acceptable to the Western Catholic Church when it is mentioned that Saint Thérèse of the Child Jesus (of Lisieux) was used as a protecting spirit against the evil spirits. St Thérèse (whom, by the way, I love) is not merely an approved protecting spirit but a canonised saint. Ingrid Sherman has related how she called on St Thérèse: 'There is a strange magnetism in those islands [the Philippines], which is conducive to greater activity of sinister psychic elements. I have frequently been under attack by black forces and once I was dragged around my room at night by an invisible entity. At another time I was visited by what sounded like a 300 pound monster bounding across the living room, coming into my bedroom and hovering over my bed, breathing heavily. In this last incident I screamed for St Theresa. I then saw a vision of her statue and heard her voice assuring me that everything would be alright.' I as a Christian know St Thérèse and have recourse to her, but how many of my fellow-Africans will not know her as their protecting spirit? Ingrid Sherman, who lived under frequent attack by evil spirits, adds: 'My saving grace was in the confidence I had built up over the years while going along the road of believing in God's forces. Cultivate the awareness that God is there and that your *spirit guides* are backing you. Then just call on God in prayer and you will receive all the help you need.' Africans have lived with spirit guides for years beyond reckoning.

Many Church intellectuals, faced with the need to interpret the ways by which God rules heaven and the heavenly beings, are puzzled when they hear that the spirits, good or bad, need permission from God to return to earth. But the intellectuals have not defined how that permission is obtained. On our side, we are certain that we have come across the good (or guardian) spirits and the bad (revenging) spirits. For instance, I have come across the spirit of Judas Iscariot — or rather, a spirit claiming to speak in his name — many times. Once I was curious to find out his identity, and he said to me: 'That Jesus lost the battle. We killed him. We speared him to death. He had no power against us.' But of course it is a lie that Jesus had no power against the arm of Judas Iscariot. The one who laughs last laughs best, and Jesus laughed at his enemies after the resurrection. They went into hiding.

For us in our area, we call the earth-bound spirits 'Ngozi' or the spirits of the witches — people who die, as they say in the Bible, without 'the bowels of mercy'. These are the hard-hearted sinners who ask God to close his Paradise to them. They got all they wanted from this earth, and enjoyed the superiority they had over many simple people. They cannot stand seeing their offspring and relatives happy. That is why they go on taking revenge, causing sickness and deaths in the family. One day we were delivering a young girl in her teens, and found afterwards that she was possessed by a relative who had died twenty-eight years before, and whose name, according to family custom, this girl had been given. The living relatives gave her the name in good faith, in order to remember the dead aunt. For many days we failed to speak to the evil spirit. However, the powers of the Lord were always pinching the spirit whenever we prayed for the girl till one day the spirit gave way and confessed: 'I am —— . This girl bears my name. Unfortunately I am here in a place of darkness, and as long as she bears this name she will have to suffer with me.' We immediately asked the evil spirit to leave her, and we told the spirit that from that time on we had changed the girl's name. We were moved to hear that the aunt's spirit was in a place of darkness, and we asked her, 'Can we help you with our prayers?' She answered: 'No need of your prayers.' We were shocked, and personally I am still shocked, to have heard such a definite 'No'.

The spirit world has to be left to those who allow themselves from time to time to be irrational. Jesus acted sometimes outside the realm of reason and of a sequential series of thought-patterns. For example, He used His spirit powers when He said to this disciples, 'Go to the village facing you, and you will

immediately find a tethered donkey and a colt with her. Untie
them and bring them to me. If anyone says anything to you, you
are to say, "The master has need of them and will send them
back directly." ' He used them, in the way of showing divine
power, when he said to the soldiers who had come to arrest him:
' "Who are you looking for?" They said, "Jesus the Nazarene".
They moved back and fell to the ground.' He also slipped out of
their grasp when they were about to stone him (John 8.59). Jesus
showed His enemies that He was not weak, and at these moments
His actions were out of the ordinary. The theologians should
have studied this power in Jesus in order to understand the irra-
tionality of the spirit-world. The Theosophical Society has this
good advice: 'Remember that though a thousand men agree
upon a subject, if they know nothing about that subject their
opinion is of no value' (Adyar, *At the feet of the Master*).

What joy we have when we know that Jesus has ethereal
powers. He is great beyond human understanding. Even while
He lived with us in human form, He was in continuous contact
with His Father in the other world, and thus when He died he
rose from the dead. The fact that He rose from the dead puts
Him higher by far than our ancestors, whose bodies still lie in
their graves. Jesus is a whole living person after the resurrection.
Our ancestors are still waiting for that big day, when they will be
wholly alive, body and soul, and once more fully themselves as
human beings, only endowed with full ethereal powers. Let us
listen to the story of the resurrection:

'On the evening of that day, the first day of the week, the
doors being shut where the disciples were, for fear of the Jews,
Jesus came and stood among them and said to them, "Peace be
with you." When he had said this, he showed them his hands and
his side. Then the disciples were glad when they saw the Lord'
(John 20. 19−20). Remark the effects of ethereal powers: the
doors were shut, but all the same 'Jesus came and stood among
them.' After spending some time with them, He went away, only
to return to confirm His resurrection to the unbelieving
Thomas: 'Eight days later, his disciples were again in the house,
and Thomas was with them. The doors were shut but Jesus came
and stood among them, and said: "Peace be with you." Then he
said to Thomas: "Put your finger here and see my hands; and
put out your hand, and place it in my side; do not be faithless,

but believing" ' (John 20. 26–7). What am I driving at? I have made my three points that Jesus is the Ancestor of ancestors, that He is the Mediator of mediators and that He is the King of the cosmos, who is available wherever He is called upon, just as He was immediately after the resurrection. Our people can therefore rely on Him because He too, like our ancestors, has the mysterious power to be present at the ancestral worship ceremonies if called upon in any way to intercede for the needs of the clan, the tribe and the whole community.

Jesus Christ is always present in His Church. After the ascension He commissioned the Holy Spirit to be the Comforter to His Church, which He founded, died for and loved with His whole being. He spent all that He had and all that He was by allowing Himself to be consumed in the Eucharist. He wanted not only to possess the members of His Church but also to become them, by being in them and with them always. He still felt that if He did not find ways and means to make His death and resurrection alive, they might be spoken about as historical facts only. Hence He commissioned the Holy Spirit to keep the faith in Him alive among the Christians, to keep His presence in the local Church ever fresh, and to ensure that His deeds for continuous realisation of the redemption of mankind should be seen by, and applied to, those who will 'hear His voice'. The Holy Spirit continues, confirms and testifies to the work of Jesus in the Christian community and in the world at large. Our people are a prepared soil for tremendous spiritual growth and maturity to sainthood in today's world.

What is man? One almost hears a voice of surprise saying 'How can you ask such a question today?' Definitions of things have changed because man's capacity for knowledge cannot always encompass in a single concept what man is. It has been said in the Bible that God regretted having created man because man does not always act rationally. He abuses his freedom and his autonomy. I, therefore, prefer to define man as William Barclay defines him: 'Man is a civil war' (*The Old and the New*). He is always at loggerheads with himself, struggling in his actions to choose between reason and folly. The Jews defined man as consisting of the twin principles of evil and goodness, the principle on the defence side being that of goodness. The Psalmist defines him as only a little below the angels, with the potentiality for integrity, purity and righteousness. But if an African is this complex thing, a 'human being', he should fully (with outsiders who have previously presumed to a monopoly in this matter) share in the complicated task of understanding himself as such. The political turmoil in Africa extinguishes the rays of hope that have formerly shone in some parts of Europe, and especially in the minds and hearts of those who spent themselves in christianising the Africans. They are bitter that things have not gone the way they hoped and expected. But in many ways these people lived in their own Africa, not in the Africa of the Africans.

The aim of Christianity is to open wide our eyes to the generosity of God to us, and to give us strength to combat the evils and adversities which make it hard for us to pursue the good shown to us by God, brought about by the redemption wrought for us by Jesus Christ. For thousands of years we have had within us an upward pull to higher things, and from time to time nurtured a vague vision of our heavenly Father. But evil forces have kept on whispering to us: 'There is no such being to whom you should have allegiance. You are yourself.' But this voice has not completely drowned the voice that continuously calls us from the origin of life — God the creator. We have been in search of God for as long as we have lived on this earth, after the fall of Adam and Eve. In many African tribes they certainly understood the nature of God as spiritual, which was how they attributed ethereal powers to the ancestors.

Like many needing to express their worship to a physical deity, Africans have had their effigies. But whatever has been the case, the effects of their worship were to be felt in their lives as individuals or as a community. For instance, a village calamity in the form of an epidemic might be said to have been caused by angry spirits or ancestors, whom they do not see but who they believe are there. They offer special prayers and sacrifices for appeasement, and the calamity is warded off; the unseen spirits have heard their prayers. The next step is a sacrifice of thanks.

The concept of God being in the heavens is what makes God to be both feared and respected. *Mwari* (Shona) means the God who is supremely great, greater even than our ancestors. In Chichewa, *Mulungu* derives from the one who creates. In the customary taking of oaths, many repeated: 'In the name of the God whose dwelling is in the sky, I swear that what I have said is true.' During the rains, when the thunderbolts were raging, it was a sign both of God's power and of his anger — 'the language of the Creator'. In the traditional African religions the names given to God show the very noble concept the people had of Him. In the Nsenga language, *Leza* means a God who is the ultimate 'Mother of Creation', the one who brings us to life and cares for us. To the Western mind this concept makes God female, but in some African traditional religions it is because life, in order to thrive and reach maturity, needs good motherly care. It is this nobility of motherhood which is emphasised. Among the Pygmies God has titles that express both fatherhood and motherhood. They depend for their lives on the forest, getting from it honey, animals, water and all that sustains them. In that sense they accept God as a mother.

Attached to the concept of 'ethereal' is not only the quality of 'agility' and *'subtilitas'*, i.e. of being able to move lightly from place to place and penetrating material substances, but also the fact of God's omnipotence. When our ancestors died they went near to God, hence they share certain powers of God, one of which, as we have seen, is the power to move with ease from place to place — e.g. the belief that the dead mother of an orphan watches her child, and sees to it that it is properly looked after. If the child is badly treated she will come to take it away by death. What makes this possible is the fact that after death she is a spirit. The dead go back to be near the Spirit-Creator who moves in the skies and on earth, and who is certainly everywhere: the omnipresence of God is reaffirmed in the following African oath: 'If what I say is a lie, may the power of God tear me to pieces.'

No one who wants to have a say in African religious affairs will win the Africans by insisting on the great achievements of Christianity. This is now a period of discovery in which Africans are trying to understand why they have been treated as they were, even by those who represented Christianity, i.e. the Christian governments. The noble work of David Livingstone, for instance, is now being coloured with some disrespect because Africans are studying the history of missionaries and mission societies and have found documents never intended for their eyes. Livingstone 'assumed that the Africans among whom he lived — and who assisted him so much in his travels across Central Africa — had *no religion*. He urged therefore that something should quickly be done "to rescue" the African's "rotting soul". To Livingstone the African was a "noble savage" and when addressing his fellow-Britons at Senate House in Cambridge on December 4, 1857, he declared: "In those romantic regions men grow wild. There dwells the negro, nature's outcast child." ' It may be that he used this language to attract attention and sympathy from the audience; however, it still remains hurtful to Africans to know that they were ever defined in such terms.

Meeting Africans in international religious consultations, one finds many who are grateful for what Christianity has achieved for the people of Africa while, on the other hand, 'but' is almost always the opening word of the next sentence: the missionaries went home satisfied with their achievement, but failed to penetrate the African soul. What a pity that quite a number of Africans who have stayed in Europe a long time have returned to Africa no longer believing. The reason is that after the regimentation of religious discipline which seemed to be imposed on them, and the show-off of the perfection of the missionaries' homeland, the Africans found their actual experience of Europe disappointing. Superstitious beliefs and occult practices are found in all nations, and cruelty and savagery are rampant in Europe no less than in 'savage continents'. Many have said 'We were deceived', but this is an exaggeration. I have heard of a professor-priest who had hours of discussion with his African former students when they went to Europe. They asked him why they had learnt 'that' at school while it was 'this' in Europe. Today several of them are no longer priests. In our modern language we say that these priests suffered from a crisis of faith. What are we going to say to the many who are now studying religious history? All we can say is that we Africans also had mistaken views of what a white man is, just as the white man has had a wrong definition of a black man. And we must all accept that none of us, black or white, has arrived at a clear concept of God. This cannot be because man is incapable of conceiving the whole essence of God. Both black and white must listen carefully to what Jesus says about His Father in Heaven. He clearly says that He is the only one who can understand His Father, and that the Father is the only one who can understand who Jesus is. The message of Christ to men of all colours is new. A missionary of today, Father John O'Donoghue, commenting on *Evangelii Nuntiandi*, says: 'The call of Christ is something quite different from the appeal of the traditional religions of mankind: it really is a new revelation, and it offers me a freedom and at the same time a hope which they could never have found by the "natural light". Christianity is not just a new and more efficient paganism; it is a new thing.'

Communication with the supernatural

As I begin to write on this subject, I feel like one who is ordered to walk barefooted on a pavement made of broken glass, and to come out of the walk unscathed. But perhaps those wanting to put me to the test know in advance that I will not succeed; the test would be asking the impossible of me. I have been asked: 'For whom do you write? Are you not in danger of seeing everyone as possessed, since you seem to believe so much in possession?' Certainly, I am not writing for those who believe that there is nothing new under the sun — though they are not excluded. At another time someone said to me: 'You know that many psychiatrists suffer in the end like their patients. Be careful, it may be the same with you.' These are seemingly the worries people have who believe that I am suffering from a delusion. Many readers of what I have written also compare my writings with those of their favourite writers. The magazine *Présence Africaine* makes this truthful comment on African writers: 'Though we have many African writers today, we cannot escape the fact that what they write is about Africa, while in their minds, as they write, their readers are the Westerners who trained them.' Another writer says that the hearts and minds of most African writers are the hearts and minds of whites. Up to this time there are thousands of Africans who are without confidence in themselves, and who cannot make their own evaluation of what they read till someone from the West has approved it. Poor Africans, when will they be themselves? When will they believe that it was never the intention of God to discriminate against them or to subject them to an endless inferiority

complex? For some of them, every step they make in the world
seems to reflect the world's judgment, 'You are the dregs of
nature', and it is impossible to convince them otherwise. So you
see how difficult it is for me to cross the pavement safely; however, I shall try to do so.

The trance

It is easy to say the word 'trance', but hard to say what goes into
it. Yoga puts some people into trances, and the cults of Hare
Krishna, the Divine Light Mission, Guru Maharaj, Brother
Julius, Sun Myung Moon and Divine Unification all claim to do
the same, so that they can believe they are in touch with the
supernatural. What kind of trances do they put the people into?
What we have called the Church of the Spirits is what we could
call each one of these cults. They have grown out of a society
which is spiritually empty, a society which adores material goods
and intellectual progress. The experience of these cults uplifts
the young to a world of their own, and they call it 'freedom'. In
the mean time they lose not only the sense of shame, courtesy
and human affection, but they also replace the true God with a
human god. This is happening also in Zambia. Many young men
and women, regardless of their denomination, are taken in
mini-buses to churches, where they experience the trance,
which is not common in their own denominations. The
authority of their parents is ignored because 'they don't know,
they are not yet with it.'

[In speaking of trance it is rather surprising that Milingo does not
mention the temporary trances or faints which often accompany healing services, although he has been criticised for allowing them to
happen. Francis MacNutt in *The Power to Heal* discusses these
phenomena, and recalls that they were common in John Wesley's services. The common expression for them is being 'slain in the spirit',
but MacNutt prefers to call it being 'overcome in the spirit', or 'resting
in the spirit', and welcomes it as a token that 'the Lord is dealing with
the problem himself.' Milingo was criticised for asking the people to sit
down during the administering of Confirmation, but he probably
learnt this precaution abroad, for MacNutt says that 'If I think that a
sufficient reason exists for not wanting people to be overcome I pray
for people in a sitting position' (p. 222). He agrees that there are
dangers of sensationalism, but believes that the reaction is so little

understood that 'the answer is not suppression — in which case its value and purpose are lost to the community — but its wise use until it becomes so well understood that its sensational aspects are minimised' (p. 214). Of his own experience in healing Milingo says: 'My body loses weight and is not subject to physical emotions. To work in this atmosphere my body is suddenly readjusted to calmness, relaxation and a unique suppleness beyond explanation. It is under the control of a power that turns it in any direction as demanded by the Lord. This power, in many instances, has remained under the orders of my will. At certain times it has gone out of me and acted beyond my expectations' (*Healing*, p. 21).]

What is a trance? It is a condition in which the human senses in the body are powerless, and the orders from the will are no longer obeyed by the living system of the physical being. Even the memory, which is an internal sense, sometimes ceases to record what is happening. In Yoga people go into a trance by their own choice, but a trance may also be forced on someone, like a 'spell', when it comes from the devil or the witches. The devil is careless: he uses his powers as soon as he is present on the scene, without preliminaries. A witch sends a spell first and acts afterwards; as we say, 'he finds it easy to make toys out of people.' The motives of both, the devil and the witch, are evil. Mostly people know what is happening when they are put into a trance by evil spirits. When they are completely controlled by the spirits, they do not remember what they say and do. One can easily distinguish the spells which come from the two sources, the witches and the devil.

A witch, in the strict sense of that word, is a person who has the power — and it is a massive power — to use what is commonly known as black magic. In other words, a witch is a person who is a faithful and committed disciple of the devil. He shares the powers of destruction which are the essential nature of the devil, which is why a witch, in this strict sense, is the devil incarnate. In his being, morality does not exist; he is geared to go against anything that is from God or is godly. Witches rarely agree to submit themselves to healing prayer, which could transform them into people who would fear God and respect His law. This is because in their formation, which often derives from heredity, they opt for the power of the devil and tell God to close his paradise. By contrast, the devil lives in a possessed person as a parasite, which is why most of the possessed go about the world looking for exorcists; they feel they have someone or something that must get rid of. Above all, they retain an element of free will, and are very conscious of their state.

The trance which puts some people in contact with the other world is no longer monopolised by the word 'ecstasy'. Many people today are in contact with the heavenly world. Many Christians have had what are called private revelations, and usually during these revelations they experience a supernatural power which has full control over them, and so they are able to communicate with the heavenly world. The effects of crossing over the human physical senses are common both to Yoga and to the spells from evil spirits. The only difference is the reason for which they are there and the source from which they come.

What is happening in the practices of the cults commonly found in Western countries which are mentioned above is that they put their clients in a permanent condition of loss of 'self', of being brainwashed. The universal belief of the Christian world in the Bible makes many of the clients of these cults easy victims. The founders and administrators of the cults choose attractive passages in the Bible and use them to suit their aims. It is true that self-denial is one condition for attaining the heights of the spirit-world, so they use this means as well. But in this case it is purposely done in order to weaken both the body and the condition of the spiritual faculties. These clients in the end are not themselves, but like automata. They seem courageous and able to face the crowd easily as they go begging and selling in the streets to raise funds. They abuse everyone as children of the devil, while they call themselves the children of God. One can admire the patience of God, who does not intervene when He sees how human beings can use His name for such a public lie. These victims are said to experience the supernatural, but what they experience is not from God. Having lost 'self-will', they become like a computer, through which a roll of what has been recorded by their memory is run gradually as they live from day to day. 'Recruits [to "the Children of God"] are starved, exhausted and harangued into a brainwashed state, then taught to hate their parents and obey the cult-leaders blindly.' They come to be in this state through abuse of the power of putting people into trances.

How do we counteract the power of Satan?

We are still dealing with what we have called 'theology of the interior', and have come to the last part. Africans are not strangers in this world. They knew, long before the coming of Christianity, how to communicate with the supernatural.

In the Lamba tribe, exorcism was carried out by tying the victim to the poles in a hut, locking him up, and pouring on the roof cold water which fell on the victim while they performed the ritual. So they had a way of fighting evil, however crude it may seem to us. Is not this the reason why people still go to the *sing'angas* or 'witch doctors' and spend days on end being exorcised? Where are the disciples of Jesus Christ who should know that they are precisely the ones whose job is to fight Satan and the effects of his lies on earth?

The Christian Church has received this power to combat the evil one and his agents from Jesus Christ: He has it permanently and His disciples have it vicariously. Jesus was a disturbing factor in any community wherein someone was possessed. The devils reacted and at times publicly confessed his divinity: 'And immediately there was in their synagogue a man with an unclean spirit; and he cried out, "What have you to do with us, Jesus of Nazareth? Have you come to destroy us? I know who you are, the Holy one of God" ' (Luke 4. 33–4). Jesus also disturbed Herod: 'King Herod heard of it, for Jesus' name had become known. Some said, "John the baptiser has been raised from the dead; that is why these powers are at work in him" ' (Mark 6. 14). When Jesus was transfigured on Mount Tabor, the three Apostles, James, John and Peter, were 'beside themselves'. They went into a trance (call it ecstasy) and experienced a tremendous joy within themselves, because they were in touch with the supernatural. This is the power Simon Magus wanted to buy from the Apostles: 'Give me also this power, that anyone on whom I lay my hands may receive the Holy Spirit' (Acts 8. 19).

It is now clear that the Africans value what they are much more than they would if they accepted without resistance the cultures and civilisations of every alien race which colonised them. In no case that I know of has a relationship on a basis of equality been realised between Africans and Christian nations. It has been believed that an African has nothing to offer in exchange for what he receives from the evangelising race, so how could he ever be equal to his master? This applies to me as well.

It is only since 1973 that I have been confided with the deep religious sentiments of my fellow Africans. Before that I used to hear a great deal of the good things I did as a priest; I received a lot of appreciation for my sermons. But today, when I am so close to the private life of thousands and thousands of Christians, I have come to realise that my fellow African Christians have much to teach me, and that many of them have direct contact with the supernatural. Some of them have come to me on their own to give me advice on most important issues which, at the time they told me about them, sounded merely casual. But when I actually passed through the period of which they spoke, then I came to know that what they had said was prophetic. To accept their advice demands humility on my part, since I was convinced that on the one hand the philosophy which I had studied opened the gates to anything intellectual, while on the other hand theology opened the gates to anything supernatural. Today I know that there is a great deal more in life that makes sense besides philosophy and theology. I also believe that in many African traditional religions there are valuable elements which satisfy reason as well as leading man to God.

To my surprise, what I condemned some years back at the beginning of my priestly ministry has been found to have 95% of good elements. It might have been true that the magnitude of evil found in the 5% of the traditional religious practices justified me in condemning it. However when I look back I feel that I asked too much from my fellow Africans. In many instances, for fear of offending me, they hid their practices from my eyes; because they were convinced that I did not understand them, they carried on their traditional religious practices secretly. This was their life and their way of approaching God, and God did not condemn them.

The method of approach on my side was wrong. Christianity is to be *lived* and not merely to be referred to. Hence it is more important to bring people to conviction than merely to show them the best of Christianity, at the cost of losing what they have and what has been in the past. People do not like to lose their identity and culture. Many traditional rituals which the Africans perform have deeper reasons than those assumed ones because of which they have been labelled 'superstitious'.

(*Plunging into Darkness*, pp. 26–44, 49–59)

4

LIVING IN CHRIST

[If the foregoing chapters show how deeply Emmanuel Milingo has been able to enter into the African mind and soul, there is no doubt whatever that his own soul is rooted in devotion to Christ, and he finds no incompatibility between his Christian and his African roots. What he has been trying to say to the Church is that in neglecting the gifts of healing, she is not being obedient to the message bequeathed to the Apostles by Christ; while preaching the miracles of the Gospel, she denies the power that is still with her.

It has not been easy in this rather polemical writing to find passages to illustrate Milingo's own deep inner life. In his humility he prefers to use quotations from Scripture, or sometimes from other writers, to illustrate the points he wants to make. In fact, in the introduction to one collection of his talks, *Father, Son and Holy Spirit*, he speaks of his reluctance to have them written down: 'I had enjoyed the scriptural inspirations I received when I gave them with only a Bible in hand. I was afraid if I wrote them down to rely on my own human inspiration . . . . I felt that the direct inspirations I used to receive as I quoted Scripture would vanish. I believed on the other hand that what people ask for might be also what God wants.'

From those talks given in America, and from two other collections — *Morality and Virtue*, given in India, and *My Call to Save the World with Jesus*, a series given to priests in Zambia — it is possible to discern the springs of Milingo's own spiritual life. The key to it is the realisation, which seems to have come to him as a revelation or conversion, that he must be more than a follower or imitator; that Christ must be *in* him. He takes seriously St Paul's words, 'It is no longer I who live, but Christ who lives in me.' So he says: 'When I took my case to a spiritual adviser he told me, "You are the mouth of the Lord. Remember that your sufferings coming from your own people should not be considered an extraordinary phenomenon. Jesus suffered at the hands of his own people." I was literally ashamed to be told this truth by my spiritual adviser, when I realised that I was standing for Jesus Christ. This lack of spiritual insight kept ringing in my conscience to emphasise the spiritual blindness which had overshadowed my soul. Slowly I came to realise the difference between being a mere instrument in

God's designs, functioning like a press-button, and a co-operative identical instrument in the divine plan. "Identical" is the word. What I want to stress is the fact that I should have been making efforts to come as close as I could to act according to the vocation God has given to me in the healing ministry' (adapted from *Healing*, p. 22).

'Identical' is perhaps not the word that everyone would use, but to Milingo it clearly denotes not only absorption or possession by Christ but also his full participation in the purpose of Christ. In another published talk, *The Divinisation of Man*, he links this to the Incarnation:]

The Incarnation

'Let us make man in our image' was the first incarnation. So we came into being, assuming physical bodies but endowed with God's image. We were created little gods, as we shared God's image. God put His Spirit into us, and accepted being with us. He bound Himself to look after and to sustain us.

The second incarnation on God's side took place when the second person, known as God the Son, became man to save fallen humanity. '*Et verbum caro factum est. Et habitavit nobis*.' He became man and lived among us. He appropriated to Himself what is ours. He did not get much from our side, except the joy that once more we were genuinely able to share His sonship. 'I am going to my Father, and to your Father.'

The third divine Incarnation is the fact of Jesus looking for ways and means to remain among us for ever. He found one way, and that was to become ordinary food for us. That was how humble He was, but He did it because He loved us. On account of love and to the measure of that love did Jesus accept the conditions of becoming man and of becoming bread or ordinary food (the Eucharist). What great incarnations God has made in order to be with us, and to sustain us in our human goals. Let us now see what we ourselves ought to do to 'divinise' ourselves into God.

To the measure that we become God, to that same measure will we accept incarnation into other people. It is from God that we understand what a fellow human is. 'Whatever you do to the least of my brothers you do it unto to me.' 'I shall not accept your sacrifice till you are reconciled to your brother. Leave then your sacrifice at the foot of the altar, and be reconciled to your brother.' The concern God has for us rightly entitles Him to be defined by Rudolf Otto as 'He Who is wholly other', in other words by His deepest nature a *sharer* of His goodness. That comes full circle to the first description of His nature in Scripture, namely Creator. 'We all', in Biblical terms, 'take our being from Him.' This includes all that exists. How much more do we need to see how God is 'wholly other'? If we, to a measure, succeeded in being also 'wholly other', even if we have little to give to others, we should have changed the world in many ways. So that if all of us Christians became little gods who by nature have the attitude of sharing, of being 'wholly other', the world today would look very different from what it is.

If I am making quick conclusions, forgive me. But I believe that even the stability of Christianity in Africa will depend on this divinisation. The way St Augustine defines charity as 'essentially directed to others' is certainly in line with Rudolf Otto. It is self-giving to those who are in need of one's services. This self-giving must also include total love for others without conditions to restrain its full outpouring. This battle against self-indulgence is the hard part of man's divinisation. Failure in this has the effects described by one of the bishops of Burundi: 'The Christianity which comes and goes in Africa reflects the foreign nature of its roots and methods. It also reflects the various national backgrounds of its missionary evangelisers, who use different methods of approach to the Apostolate.' These are the effects of the failure of the divinisation of humanity. God allows Himself to become everything, but never destroys the identity of the things in which He merges.

Archbishop Mihayo of Tabora defined incarnation at the 1970 study conference of AMECEA (the Association of Member Episcopal Conferences of Eastern Africa): 'If the incarnational principle — or principle of adaptation, if you will — means anything at all to us, it would mean that we become truly ourselves, that we localise, that we try to be as self-reliant as possible.' (*Divinisation of Man*, pp. 5−6)

[In *Father, Son and Holy Spirit* Milingo makes an eloquent assertion of personal commitment to Christ reminiscent of John Wesley, and of a kind which in other saints of the Christian Church has been rewarded by the special gifts which Milingo appears to have.]

Personal testimony

I would like to share with you my personal relation with Jesus, instead of preaching to you about Him. I will tell you of my own belief and trust in Jesus Christ. From the experience of my Charismatic life since 1973, I have come to know that Jesus is my personal saviour. By this I do not want to say that He is only a saviour to me; no, for you too, each one of you, Jesus is your personal saviour.

I have come to realise that I have a very powerful saviour. I have also come to know that not only was Jesus involved in my salvation, but that He brought me into being, He created me: 'In the beginning was the Word: the Word was with God and the Word was God. He was with God in the beginning. Through him all things came to be, not one thing had its being but through him' (John 1. 1–3). I know, just as you too know, that this Word is none other than Jesus Christ. I feel so much about Jesus, but I also feel that you and I do not sufficiently publicise Jesus and His works. Listen to the same gospel: 'But to all who did accept him he gave power to become children of God, to all who believe in the name of him who was born not out of human stock or urge of the flesh or will of man but of God himself' (John 1. 12–14). This to me means a lot.

It is Jesus who has shared His Sonship with me, which is why I am today a child of God. Just as 'through him all things came to be' — meaning through Jesus Christ who is known as the Word of God — I find here that my second sonship as a child of God has also been worked out through Jesus Christ and by Jesus Christ. First, I was created through Him. God uttered a word in order that I should be created, and that word was Jesus Christ, the word of God, and so I came into being. Again, after my ancestors Adam and Eve sinned, it is through the incarnation of Jesus Christ that I am able once again to say I am a child of God. As at the beginning God said 'Let us make man in our own image' and a man came into being, the same thing happened when we had sinned. God said, 'Let us save man from his misery,' and so in Jesus God Himself became man in order to re-create me. This is how today I am able to be called a child of God. My dear brothers and sisters, see how Jesus is involved in my life.

I am not making a useless statement when I say that to me Jesus Christ is everything, and I look at Christianity as being defined in Jesus Christ and being complete in Jesus Christ because Jesus did not just come to make us specialists in Christianity, but to make us like Himself — Christ-like. Therefore Christianity *is Christ* and must be so to anyone who will ultimately be a genuine Christian, a Christian who deserves the name. As He Himself says, 'I am the Way, the Truth and the Life. No one can come to the Father except through me. If you know me, you know my Father too. From this moment you know him and have seen him' (John 14. 6−7). To me Jesus is everything; outside these three words by which Jesus called himself — the way, the truth and the life — there is nothing I need. If Jesus truly becomes the way in my life, the way to my Father, I am certain that I will arrive because He knows where His father lives. If Jesus is the truth, and if I abide by the truth which he has preached, I know that I will not make mistakes. I am protected by Him from error. Finally, if Jesus is the life, what else do I need? It means I have everything. Jesus himself says further on, 'No one can come to the father except through me.' With these words, I know that I am in the right path to the Father. I want to go to the Father and I am doing it through Jesus Christ. He will do the paving of the way to the Father for me, so I just have to follow Him.

Once we have accepted His message, He grants the continuous flow of life in us. He unites us to himself to be sure that we are kept alive, hence 'I am the true vine, and my Father is the vinedresser. Every branch in me that bears no fruit he cuts away, and every branch that does bear fruit he prunes to make it bear even more. You are pruned already, by means of the word that I have spoken to you. Make your home in me, as I make mine in you. As a branch cannot bear fruit all by itself, but must remain part of the vine, neither can you unless you remain in me. I am the vine, you are the branches. Whoever remains in me, with me in him, bears fruit in plenty: for cut off from me you can do nothing. Anyone who does not remain in me is like a branch that has been thrown away — he withers; these branches are collected and thrown on the fire, and they are burnt' (John 15. 1−6). Here Jesus says that He is Himself the stock of life, the life that flows from Him to us. If we are branches, it means our whole lives are holy, and our spiritual life is being fed by Him and comes from Him. It is here that we can understand the transformation a Christian needs after accepting the messages of Christ. We are Christians to the measure that we work hand in hand with Christ; we are Christians to the measure that we open up channels in ourselves through which this life of Christ flows into us, and as such we therefore become replicas of Jesus Christ. Then truly we can say with Jesus that we are his branches. And 'as a branch cannot bear fruit all by itself but must remain part of the vine,' neither can you unless you remain in Him.

Growth in Christ

We are able, in life, to change a lemon into an orange through the scientific system of grafting an orange branch on to a lemon tree. That grafting means cutting away lemon branches and replacing them with orange branches, which are the only ones that we then allow to come out. If out of that orange branch some fractions of the lemon branches grow, we cut them away, and go on working on that new shoot till there are no more signs of the lemon tree. The fruit it bears must taste sweet, not bitter or sour. Then we know that our work has been successful. When we have become Christ-like, and thus truly deserve to be called Christians, the work that has been done in us through the Holy Spirit is exactly like that of grafting an orange branch on to a lemon tree. It means that we give up our old ways.

We must be gentle-hearted, smooth in manners, full of love for our brothers and sisters — in a word, we must be as sweet as Jesus Christ. All that is the reflection of bitterness and sourness belongs to the old way. It has been taken away in baptism. We are now truly a new creation. What St Paul says to the Ephesians is very appropriate for us here on earth: 'You must give up your old way of life; you must put aside your old self, which gets corrupted by following illusory desires. Your mind must be renewed by a spiritual revolution so that you can put on the new self that has been created in God's way, in the goodness and holiness of the truth' (Eph. 4. 22—4). A Christian who does not become what St Paul describes here is certainly not a Christian. Jesus means it when He says 'I am the vine, you are the branches', and He does not expect us to deviate from this truth. If we have not missed the truth, then let us accept that our life has to be grafted on to Jesus Christ. This is how we can truly be the branches.

But remember that at the beginning of the Church Paul himself was anti-Christ. He could not stand the name of the Church that had been established by Jesus Christ. On the other hand, why not admire the miracle that has been worked in St Paul? How could he, who was not among the Apostles and was never in the company of Jesus Christ during His life, change so much as truly to deserve the name of being an Apostle?

To me St Paul is a concrete example of what grace can do in a human being, and his life proves that God has no favourites. If one co-operates with God, one will go through life with success even if one comes across many difficulties as St Paul did. St Paul's ambition is also my ambition, and we find what it was in the letter to the Philippians: 'All I want is to know Christ and the power of his resurrection and to share his sufferings by reproducing the pattern of his death. That is the way I can hope to take my place in the resurrection of the dead' (Phil. 3. 10−11). As I said at the beginning, St Paul's rootedness in Jesus is my own ambition. How I wish that it becomes yours as well!

I know Christ and the power of His resurrection; and I wish to share His sufferings by recreating the pattern of His death in me. I am not looking at Jesus only through the eyes of the triumphant resurrection; I would like to follow Christ in His moments of depression, disappointment and discouragement. I know that as a human being it is hard to behave well when facing these moments, but as my ambition is to be grafted on to Christ, I hope that as He sustains my whole life, He sustains me in the life of joy as well as in the life of sorrow. It is through suffering that I can show a proper balance in evaluating what is given to me and what is not given to me. It is through suffering that I will prove my detachment from the things which otherwise take me away from the love of Christ. I would like one day to be able to dare to say these words of St Paul: 'But because of Christ I have come to consider all these advantages that I had as disadvantages. Not only that, but I believe nothing can happen that will outweigh the supreme advantage of knowing Christ Jesus my Lord. For him I have accepted the loss of everything, and I look on everything as so much rubbish if only I can have Christ and be given a place in him. I am no longer trying for perfection by my own efforts, the perfection that comes from the Law: but I want only the perfection that comes through faith in Christ, and is from God and based on faith' (Phil. 3. 7–9). I must accept Jesus as a whole: Jesus of the resurrection, and Jesus of the crucifixion and death. Having been grafted on to Jesus, I must have both sides of His life reproduced in me.

I admire St Paul. Listen to his advice to Timothy, given at a time when he was already in prison. He shows no bitterness towards his enemies who mistreated him; instead he would like Timothy to rejoice, and even to boast of him as his leader, who is in prison for the sake of Jesus. 'That is why I am reminding you now to fan into a flame the gift that God gave you when I laid my hand on you. God's gift was not a spirit of timidity, but the spirit of power, and love, and self-control. So you are never to be ashamed of witnessing to the Lord, or ashamed of me for being his prisoner: but with me bear the hardships for the sake of the Good News, relying on the power of God who has saved us and called us to be holy — not because of anything we ourselves have done but for his own purpose and by his own grace. This grace has already been granted to us, in Christ Jesus, before the beginning of time, but it has only been revealed by the appearing of our saviour Christ Jesus. He abolished death, and he has proclaimed life and immortality through the Good News; and I have been named its herald, its apostle and its teacher' (II Timothy 1. 6–11). In this letter St Paul is encouraging Timothy, relying on the power of God, to be ready to receive, as he says, the hardships for the sake of the goodness. Paul accepted Jesus whole. It is this that all we Christians should know: that as Christians we are expected to be the true reflection of Jesus Christ, which means that in our life Jesus has to be shown — the suffering servant as well as, later, the triumphant resurrected Jesus.

The command to love

What we have said about sharing the sonship with Jesus Christ means that we should also do things that Jesus Christ does. Jesus has lived on earth with us, having come to do the will of His Father. He was sent to come and save us. We know how emphatic He was to all of us, when He was living, on the question of abiding by what He commanded us: for instance, He says to His Apostles what also applies to us: 'What I command you is to love one another' (John 15. 17). In His command of love Jesus said that this should be the sign of all His disciples. If this is an order and if we truly love Him, we should abide by what He tells us to do.

The world lacks this love that we are talking about. We must learn to love one another, and tending to perfection means nothing else but the relation and the love we ought to have for one another. We should wish one another well, we should serve one another, we should respect one another. If we do all this, and do it in Jesus' name, then we are Christians. Jesus himself says: 'I give you a new commandment: love one another; just as I have loved you, you also must love one another. By this love you have for one another, everyone will know that you are my disciples.' If all Christians in the whole world really loved Jesus and obeyed his commands, then this world would be a very different place.

Tending to perfection means learning to love as Jesus loves everybody. It is through love that we can bear many problems. It is through love that we can lay down our lives for others. It is through love that we appreciate other people's talents and gifts as the work of God in them. When Jesus Himself says 'Be perfect as my Father is perfect', it is an invitation to love. Jesus has loved us so much that He offers us all that He has and even wants us to be so ambitious as to become perfect as His heavenly Father is perfect. But what is His Father other than the one who is defined as love? He brought all of us into being because He loves us. Let us work hard to imitate the life of Christ, which is the life of love. Then we shall find that Jesus Christ is love itself. He came to save us because He loves us, and He wants us to love as He loves, even to go so far as to lay down our lives for our brothers and sisters. In this love of Christ for the human race, each one of us is included. Jesus did not love an abstract humanity removed from the individual's needs. He laid down his life for each one of us. That is why we read in the parable which He Himself gave that a good shepherd will leave ninety-nine out of his hundred sheep and look for the hundredth which is lost. He leaves all the rest which are safe and will risk suffering himself the same difficulties as the lost sheep may have passed through, and will struggle to save it. Then he brings it back to the fold and his joy is complete. We

also read about the conversion of a single sinner and He says that
not only are the people on earth happy but also even the saints
and angels are happy that one single sinner has repented.

Remember then your own conversion, your own day of baptism, your own change of heart and mind, the day when you
committed your life to the Lord. You can imagine how much
Jesus rejoiced with the angels and saints. You alone, as an individual, caused Jesus great joy. Therefore do not just believe that
Jesus died for humanity in the abstract; He died for you as an
individual. Remember that on the day you were converted, that
you were baptised, and that you committed your life to the
Lord — on that day all attention was on you. He left the ninety-
nine to fend for themselves, because He felt they were secure and
did not need His attention at that time, and was there to see to it
that you had all that you needed to become truly a child of God.
So Jesus loves you as an individual. Jesus died for you as an individual. Jesus feeds you as one branch attached to him who is the
vine. You too have the right to call Jesus your personal saviour.

From the outset, I would like to explain the two terms which I
use in describing my personal relation with the Holy Spirit: 'my
life' and 'my guide'. Let me present to you first what St Paul says:
'Your interests, however, are not in the unspiritual, but in the
spiritual, since the Spirit of God has made his home in you. In
fact, unless you possessed the Spirit of Christ you would not
belong to him. Though your body may be dead it is because of
sin, but if Christ is in you then your spirit is life itself because you
have been justified; and if the Spirit of him who raised Jesus from
the dead is living in you, then he who raised Jesus from the dead
will give life to your own mortal bodies through his Spirit living
in you' (Romans 8. 9 – 11). My brothers and sisters, I believe that
having been baptised, I have become the brother of Jesus and
the son of God. I have become the brother of Jesus because I
have received the Spirit of Christ by which I am sealed and which
makes me a child of God. Through the Holy Spirit I am transformed into a child of God and if this is so, then the Holy Spirit is
my life. May I once more quote St Paul's letter to the Romans:
'Everyone moved by the Spirit is a son of God. The Spirit you
received is not the spirit of slaves bringing fear into your lives
again; it is the spirit of sons, and it makes us cry out, "*Abba*,
Father!" The Spirit himself and our spirit bear united witness

that we are children of God. And if we are children we are heirs
as well: heirs of God and co-heirs with Christ, sharing his suffering so as to share his glory' (Romans 8. 9–11). This in short is
what I mean when I say the Holy Spirit is my life.

(Father, Son and Holy Spirit, pp. 9–18)

[The way to attain oneness with Christ and the presence of the Holy
Spirit is clearly through prayer, and Milingo gives some account of his
experience of prayer as a living, flowing and continuous force, rather
than any set form:]

Prayer

The things which we neglect. I am here to talk about prayer. I
am certain that you all know what prayer is, and you teach it so
often to the faithful. In order that I may not repeat what you
know, I am going to define prayer in a different way. I am going
to emphasise the point of being in prayer and moving with
prayer. I would not like to go back to my seminary life, which
divided my prayer life into vice and virtue, mortal sin and venial
sin, sins of omission and commission, etc. These distinctions
developed within me a confusion which would have led me to
scrupulosity. Because of these distinctions my prayer life was
categorised into omission and commission, while some of the
prayers omitted came to be mortal sins or venial sins. In my
effort to avoid mortal sins and even venial sins, I lost the object
for which I was saying the prayers. My greatest puzzle was that I
did not know who had the scale by which to categorise my
prayers into omission and commission, mortal sin and venial sin.
I personally had no scale to weigh my neglected prayers. Fortunately the burden was finally left in the hands of my confessor
who gave me penance accordingly. My duty to pray was sum-
marised into two parts:
(1) To recite during the day all the prayers alloted to me as a
priest. These were the Breviary, the Rosary, meditation and the
Mass. Each of these weighed accordingly into a mortal sin or a
venial one if not said within the twelve hours from noon to
midnight.
(2) I had the impression that there was no better prayer than
those on the list. Someone thought over them, and included in
them all the needs of humanity as a whole and as individuals.

This left me without a target. My worry was to recite the prayers, regardless of my disposition to say them. The result was that for many years I recited these prayers *ex opere operato* (i.e. as a received formula, or as a professional duty, the results to come automatically) not *operantis* (i.e. as a true participator), and so gained very little from them. It took me years to become aware that prayers are directed to someone living. He is not satisfied merely to listen to a voice reciting the prayers, but is interested in the person who produces the voice and who should put his or her spirit in the prayers which are being recited. He goes to the source of the voice, and often questions the suppliant: 'Do you mean it?' But as we don't often listen to Him, we go on reciting our prayers as a duty and routine. How can we put our spirit in a prayer where the emphasis is on its being a law? It should not be taken as a law, but as a way of life. If we are aware of the fact that we are addressing someone who is a living person, we are then able to add our own personal prayers when we feel that we would like to push our petitions further than what is being said in this routine fixed prayer.

May I dare to say that what makes a saint is not the recitation of fixed prayers but rather the habit of prayer. We must move in prayer and with prayer. For us as we grow into Christ, we must be aware of His presence within us to such an extent that prayer should be an established relationship between Him and ourselves. It is possible that theologians have not yet coined a word to express this established relationship, but all the same it is a fact that this kind of prayer is a bond of intimacy with Christ, a continuous relationship between Christ and the soul that is possessed by Him. That is what I consider to be the prayer that really sanctifies. When this is so, all the other prayers come in as strenghtening elements of this intimacy and union with Christ, which will be said not by force of law but rather because having accepted Christ these prayers are a means to an end. They are categorised into prayers of praise, of thanksgiving, of petition, of repentance and so on, which present to Him my many needs. As I recite them my dispositions respond according to the need mentioned. I reach a stage when I no longer consider prayer as a way to punishment if omitted (sin) or a way to a reward if recited in time (virtue); it is a way to an intimate union of knowledge and love, and a sustenance of my commitment to Christ.

I have opted to differ from the common definition of prayer as 'a conversation with God', because the word 'conversation' has a very light meaning, as if (so I imagine it) the suppliant has met God on His way to the house of angels. I don't know where the suppliant is coming from, but they greet each other and hold a casual conversation, an exchange of courtesies. On the contrary, prayer does not consist only in conversing with God, unless this means merely being in contact with God. If we have really been transformed by the message of Christ and can sincerely say '*Abba*, Father' to our Heavenly Father, we should no longer just converse with God, but rather be with God every minute of every hour of every day. This presence of God within us will bring with it a permanent communion between God and ourselves. A baby, though still unable to speak, is aware of the importance of the mother, and there exists between the baby and the mother a relationship which is internal and is only seen externally from time to time. Prayer should lead us to this permanent communion with God, which develops into love and puts away the idea of prayer as a law.

Prayer confirms the soul's response to the divine touch of love. In this case to pray means to put myself with my whole being in the embracing love of God. Like a baby who feels safe in the presence of the mother, so should be my dispositions when I am in prayer. It is as if I am walking in light surrounded by darkness. During this time I am communing with my beloved Father. I am consulting Him, I am listening to Him, I am reporting to Him about my duties and I am presenting to Him my needs and those of the brothers and sisters I serve. As I walk away from this active communion, I still retain within me the awareness that He is with me as I go to the battlefield to save my people from the claws of the evil one. He is there backing me up, and assuring me that I will return victorious.

What is prayer, you are still asking? It is to be with God, to move with God, to consult Him, to listen to Him and to act with Him. Prayer is the life of a Christian, still more of a priest. It is how a Christian remains a Christian, a child of God. Mother Teresa has said: 'It is not possible to engage in a direct apostolate without being a soul of prayer. . . . Our activity is truly apostolic only in so far as we permit Him to work in us and through us, with His power, with His desire, with His love. We must become holy, not because we want to feel holy, but because Christ must be able to live His life fully in us . . . Prayer enlarges the heart until it is capable of containing God's gift of Himself ' (quoted in M. Muggeridge, *Something Beautiful for God*).

Don't be surprised that I have preferred to dwell longer on what prayer is than on its importance. Prayer is to a Christian like the oil that prolongs the durability of a machine. Someone says prayer is as necessary as breathing is to us. That is to say, we can't live without breathing. Hence we can't spiritually live without prayer.

(*My Call to Save the World with Jesus*, pp. 15–18)

[In an address in New Delhi in 1979, Milingo, clearly taking into account the Eastern tradition of meditation, and encouraged by it, went still more deeply into prayer as communication with God:]

It is not necessary to call the whole human race to one place and to prove to the people that they have missed their goal. What will turn the clock back to the starting point is experience of communion with the Supreme Being. The majority of the human race have overfed themselves on the rubbish of worldly goods. They cannot stand on their own feet. It is only by mercy of the Supreme Being that they can once more lift up their eyes to Him their Creator, and once more find their way to Him. Hence the psalmist rightly prays, 'Arise Lord, come to our aid, our stomachs have been stuck in the ground.' It means that we have been feeding ourselves on the wrong food, and have poisoned ourselves. Hence the misery which surrounds us. We need to be helped to stand on our feet, and to begin the march towards God our Creator and Supreme Father.

God, as He created us, never intended us to be self-sufficient. He wanted us to be together with Him, and to share love, joy, peace and unity forever. But we all know the story of the coming into our being of Māyā, the origin of vice. Adam and Eve did it all, and cut what was a natural communion with God, which now has to be searched for and acquired. There are within us strings which pull us towards God. But in some people they are very weak, and in others almost non-existent, due to the fact that they are brought up in circumstances dominated by materialism. The values stressed in such societies are earthly joy, happiness, prestige, popularity and so on, which as a matter of fact are not realised. Without referring to the Supreme Being, these values are attained through egoism, self-aggrandisement and injustice, and at the cost of others suffering. Even if by any chance such people may be religious in one way or another, religion may only be ritualistic and ceremonial. They may have no internal obligations or commitment to what they believe. If they have not changed internally, they still remain pagan and non-religious.

It is important to teach people not only to know God but also to communicate with Him. The aim of this communication must not just be a seeking of spiritual consolation, but rather the coming to a realisation that God, being our Father, is certainly in touch with us. We know that on His side He is always in touch with us. It is on our side that a corresponding reciprocal communication is lacking. This communication when realised will remind us that we are citizens of the other world, in which — when we shall be with Him, our Father and Creator — we shall be completely ourselves.

We have within us the wound of deviation, which pulls us down to earthly things; but communion with God sustains us, uplifts us from the mire of sin, and dispels from our minds and hearts the spiritual blindness which comes from the wound of deviation. We call this internal weakness the wound of deviation, because it continually pulls us away from the right path, blinds our judgement and tries to flatter us by giving us short-lived material satisfactions. It is like a merchant who goes to any length to advertise his wares on the roadside so that the passers-by will buy them all. He does all he can to prove that he has the best wares, and that there is nothing better in the supermarkets and wholesale stores. But he does this for his own profit, not for the benefit of the customers. If they go to the source of the wares in wholesale stores or supermarkets, they will have a bigger choice and will find all they want. The wound of deviation stops us on the way, and makes us believe that what matters is all that is in this world. How many human beings have failed to reach the full store of eternal goods, where they will have everything to their full satisfaction and of their own choice.

Even as we reach a stage of habitually communicating with the Supreme Father, we should not wish to die and be suddenly united to Him. This is running away from our responsibility to share with our brothers and sisters our celestial experiences. When our time comes, He will release us from the chores of this earthly life, and cover us with the clothes of the spirit world, which the influence of the wound of deviation cannot penetrate. I do not believe that we can cause a change in today's world and save it from its headlong plunge into self-destruction unless we feed the minds and hearts of its citizens with the spiritual values. We must not stop at an accumulation of knowledge of spiritual values, but rather go on to reach their hearts and minds, to the extent of accepting the supremacy of spiritual over material values. When the citizens of this world realise this and begin to commune with the Supreme Father, they will then be able to strike a balance in the evaluation of their needs. They will not rush to a heap of wealth, they will not take sex as the sole end of their existence, nor will they boast of their power as if they can lift the earth. In everyone there are inadequacies and limitations, and so there will be until we arrive at the goal of life, which is — as most people of all persuasions believe — personal fulfilment; although personal fulfilment can only be obtained in God, the Supreme Being.

Communication with the spirit world

Let us put aside the discoveries of the spirit world in contact with this earth. These are facts beyond doubt, and many books have been written on the matter. Some years back, I told a group of priests that I was able to speak with the dead and the evil spirits. They almost uttered the word '*Anatemasit*', meaning 'May he be cursed,' but because I was their Ordinary in charge of an archdiocese, it was hard for the priests to excommunicate me. I kept quiet. Later I produced four pamphlets on my experiences with the spirit world. I have never come across any Western missionary who has accepted what I have written about the spirit world, which in my pamphlets is entitled 'the world-in-between'. Therefore I have written very little of those experiences because, in charity, I do not want to disturb their beliefs and their mental patterns. However, it would be a lie on my part to deny facts in order to please them. I do not have the power to share my experiences with them. Such experiences are not easily transplanted to a mind which is totally closed to the

acceptance of ways of approaching the spirit world that are
prevalent in other cultures. I read the book of Prajapita Brahma
Kumaris, *Moral Values, Attitudes and Moods*, with complete
ease, and understood everything. There were indeed a few
things which are unfamiliar in my religious beliefs, but that did
not prevent me from understanding. Why is it that your presen-
tation of thoughts and religious beliefs is so easily understood by
me? It is because I have passed through the experiences you talk
about. I have also an open attitude of mind to take in other people's ways of approach to religious beliefs.

Let me come back to communication with the spirit world. I
do not want you to think that my contacts with it are operated
like those of mediums. No, I can contact the dead on my own, or
through a sick person who is being harassed by evil or revenging
spirits. Sometimes these spirits are from the family, the members
who died; but when they are spirits of revenge, it is clear that it is
not well with them up there. That is to say that they are paying
for their bad lives on earth, and hence they are roaming the
earth joining hands with the evil one, Satan. So when I discover
who they are, I proceed to cast them out.

I have also found out that many evil spirits take noble names,
such as those of famous men, chiefs, kings, presidents and so on.
Thus they want to be honoured, and so when they possess
people, they permeate those people with their norms of living.
They formulate rules for them such as 'Don't go to church to
pray; don't eat pork, fish, cassava, chicken etc. Use cooking pots
in which no other food, except yours, will be cooked. From now
on you are married to us. You are ours, never accept your boy-
friend/girl-friend. Follow our ritual and dance the dance of the
lions, the snakes, the monkeys, the spirits etc.' These people lead
lives of hardship, which take them out of ordinary life. They are
perpetually sick, since in them are living entities from another
world. It is because these entities are parasites in people that I
use the power of God to speak to them and cast them out. I share
this power and authority from Jesus Christ the Messiah to cast
out the evil spirits and the spirits of revenge. 'The seventy-two
came back rejoicing. "Lord", they said, "even the devils submit
to us when we use your name." He said to them, "I watched
Satan fall like lightning from Heaven. Yes, I have given you
power to tread underfoot serpents and scorpions and the whole

strength of the enemy; nothing shall ever hurt you" ' (Luke 10.
17–20).

For seven years I have waged war against the evil spirits. It has
been a hard war. They have used all sorts of methods to harm
me, but my spirit which never goes to bed is always on the alert to
protect me. The evil spirits are aware that if they succeed in putting me into a trance, they would then make a mockery of me.
They would pinch me, twist my body and abuse my imagination
by bringing all sorts of pictures to my mind. Slowly then they
would put into me the spirit of fear. This is what they cannot succeed in doing to me. When my body is at rest, I am all the
same — to use Brahma Kumaris' term — 'soul-conscious'.
That is why in the middle of the night, while I am asleep, if the
evil spirits come and attack me, I will wake up and send them
away with a blessing or the sign of the cross. Then I go back to
sleep.

The fact is that there is never a time when I am alone, even as I
am speaking now. I am in the company of many guardians
whose ranks I don't know. I am grateful to them all, for they
have protected me on several occasions from the evil spirits and
the spirits of revenge. They have been at my side as I travelled to
distant places and lands. They are immediately at my side when
I call upon them. They have lifted me up out of depressions and
discouragements. They have been the most cherished friends to
me. They have waged a harder war against the evil spirits than I
have done, feeble human being as I am. It is for this reason that I
am so grateful to them all. I should stop discussing this matter
here, although I have many examples to give you.

Communion with God

The aim of attaining communion with our Supreme Father
should be that of filling this world with His spirit. Man, having
been given the greatest privilege on this planet to be king of creation, should be always anxious to know the latest news from the
Supreme Father, to whom he has to render an account of his
duties. We are not complaining of the behaviour of elephants in
India, buffaloes in Africa, kangaroos in Australia or sheep in
France. Nobody would listen to such complaints. Our expectation of good behaviour is from our fellow-men. The cruelties

which fill this world in the form of wars, imprisonments, death squads, torture etc. are all brought about by human beings who know very little of the behaviour of their Supreme Father. In many cases they are people who know only about their own welfare, and nobody else exists outside themselves.

But to commune with God is not easy. While God as our creator continuously lavishes on us all the good we need, He does not force us to discover Him from within ourselves. For us to regain what we lost through Adam and Eve, it will be necessary to make our own personal efforts. 'Regaining' here does not mean just acquiring once again the goods we lost, but much more. We ourselves must once more be polished and become clean and innocent as we were in Adam and Eve before they sinned. To come back to this state, we have to be transformed into new creatures, even as we lead this earthly life. Brahma Kumaris entitles this 'surrender to God'. He explains it as follows: 'The most effective means of eradicating vices and demoniac tendencies is to be dedicated or surrendered wholeheartedly to Him who is the supreme soul. Without any hesitation, i.e. without thinking too much of what I am at present, I should consider that from this moment nothing is mine, but what "I" and "mine" stood for once have now been all surrendered to Him. I have now firmly to feel that body, mind and everything are His and now I have to use these as He directs.'

This is what I term 'exchange of rights' between God and man. This is far from being a universal ambition among human beings. God cannot therefore show all that He has on His side to a person who has just a relationship of being a creature. It is not enough. We are noble beings, free beings, intelligent beings. We must decide and choose our way of life. It is up to us to search for the best way to be children of God, so that we can truly call Him 'Father'. The way is through purification, integrity of life and communing with our Supreme Father. St Paul says this on the matter: 'What God wants is for you all to be holy. He wants you to keep away from fornication, and each one of you to know how to use the body that belongs to him in a way that is holy and honourable, not giving way to selfish lust like the pagans who do not know God. . . . We have been called by God to be holy, not to be immoral' (I. Thess. 4. 3−8).

Jesus, the founder of Christianity, though He was the son of

God, did not dispense Himself from mortification of the body. As a preparation to His public mission to bring the Good News of salvation to mankind, He went to the desert and fasted for forty days and nights. He ate nothing during that time to prove to His followers who were to become His disciples that 'man does not live by bread alone,' as He answered the evil one who had put Him to the test over the necessity of food: 'Jesus returned from the Jordan full of the Holy Spirit and was led by the spirit into the desert, where He was tempted by the devil for forty days. In all that time He ate nothing, so that He was hungry when it was over. The devil said to Him, "If you are God's son, order this stone to turn into bread." But Jesus answered, "The scripture says, man cannot live by bread alone" ' (Luke 4. 1−4).

Matthew's Gospel not only says 'Man cannot live by bread alone' but adds that he 'needs every word that God speaks' (Matthew 4. 4). The devil tempted Jesus in other matters such as wealth and worldly glory, but He still rejected everything, and sent the evil one away. During that period when He was hungry, the devil thought that it was the best time to ask Him to demonstrate His powers, and prove that He was the Son of God. But the devil did not realise that Jesus was feeding on God's words and was therefore spiritually fit, and this was what mattered. He had full control over His body, and so the devil could not reach His soul through the bodily temptations.

Our master Jesus was always out-going ['wholly other'] as He lived on earth. He was undoubtedly someone without sin. He faced His enemies and asked them: 'Can anyone of you accuse me of sin?' Even Pilate, in His last moments, searched for a crime in our Master's behaviour and there was none. They tortured Him, mocked Him, whipped, slapped and spat on Him, and during all this suffering He uttered no word in the form of an insult or a curse. He bore everything on His body, but had full control over it. We read in the Holy Scripture: 'Pilate called together the chief priests, the leaders, and the people, and said to them, "You brought this man to me and said that he was misleading the people. Now, I have examined him here in your presence, and I have not found him guilty of any of the crimes you accuse him of." Nor did Herod find him guilty, for he sent him back to us. There is nothing this man has done to deserve death. So I will have him whipped and let him go' (Luke 23. 13−16).

'Then Pilate took Jesus and had him whipped. The soldiers made a crown of thorny branches and put it on his head; then they put a purple robe on him and came to him and said, "Long live the King of the Jews!" And they went up and slapped him' (John 19. 1–3). During all this time Jesus had full control of Himself. Despite what He felt in His soul and on His body, He bore everything for the salvation of the human race. Instead of retaliating, answering back or making efforts to prove Himself innocent, His goodness and love for others was still shown at such a peak of pain and anguish. As He hung on the cross, He was heard saying, 'Forgive them, for they know not what they do.' One of the criminals hanging on his own cross on Calvary, where Jesus was crucified, said to Him: 'Remember me, Jesus, when you come as king.' Jesus said, 'I promise you that today you will be in Paradise with me' (Luke 23. 42–44). Look how much He was concerned about others. While He had no sins of His own He bore them on our behalf. He was perfect and was able truly to remain constantly in touch with God. Both body and soul were totally surrendered to God; as He often said, 'I do the will of Him who sent me.' He said to Philip the Apostle, 'Believe me when I say that I am in the Father and the Father is in me. The Father, who remains in me, does his own work' (John 14. 11).

Merely to wish to commune with God for a short time, without the aim of remaining continuously in His presence, may only give human consolation. Communing with God must have roots within the soul, and from these roots will radiate God's light and, slowly, a permanent and intimate relationship between God and ourselves, finally reaching a stage where we will strive to identify ourselves with God. If we then will reach this stage already here on earth, we will be blessed with the consequences of deification, which are righteousness, integrity, purity, love, joy, freedom of the children of God, peace, brotherhood, unity and harmony. But we must first purify ourselves of the following vices as enumerated by our Master Jesus: 'It is what comes out of a person that makes him unclean. For from inside, from a person's heart, come the evil ideas which lead him to do immoral things, to rob, kill, commit adultery, be greedy, and do all sorts of evil things: deceit, indecency, jealousy, slander, pride and folly — all these evil things come from inside a person and make him unclean' (Mark 7. 20–3). There is no chance of being numbered among the sages, saints and mystics when one is in fact merely driven to learn the science of the saints by human curiosity. God is light, and those who desire to be in contact with Him must first of all get rid of all that our Master Jesus has enumerated above. This is what is demanded of the Yogi by Prajapita Brahma Kumaris: 'It is continence that purifies one's mind, sharpens one's sense of right understanding and brings to man that spiritual strength which helps him to conquer vices and to endure and face the difficulties that crop up in the way of his communion with God' (*How to make life blissful and worth diamonds*).

Looking at the prayers of the Jews in the form of psalms, one admires their familiarity with God. Their God seemed to be so near, and they used to address Him directly. One also admires how they accepted Him as the cause of everything and hence they make Him responsible for calamities and misfortunes as well as joy and victory. When they wished good or evil, they said it all to God. Listen to this: 'Evil men go wrong all their lives; they tell lies from the day they are born. They are full of poison like snakes; they stop up their ears like a deaf cobra, which does not hear the voice of the snake-charmer or the chant of the clever magician. Break the teeth of these fierce lions, O God. May they disappear like water draining away; may they be crushed like weeds on a path. May they be like snails that dissolve into slime; may they be like a baby born dead that never sees light' (Psalm 58). They were certainly violent in their prayers (Jesus our Master never cursed a person, or wished anyone evil); however, here I wish only to show how the Jews addressed God so familiarly and directly. They were certainly in contact with God in many ways. They had many prophets among them, and God also used to speak to them as a community through Moses on Mount Sinai and in the tent during their forty years' sojourn in the desert.

Paul the Apostle said that he once went into ecstasy, and was in the third Heaven where he saw things beyond description. He says, 'Eyes have not seen, ears have not heard, nor has it entered man's heart to understand what God has prepared for those who love him.' We can presume that this happened during prayer, as he was in touch with God. He was given a foretaste of the life to come. He was a man of faith.

In the Catholic Church there are many contemplative orders, who have chosen to be always at prayer. These have a thousand experiences of their ecstatic union with God. In some of these orders are found mystics whose earthly lives are already almost in union with the Heavenly One. But I would like a proportion of this ecstatic union with God to be taught to ordinary people, since we are all the children of God. When our Master Jesus said 'Be perfect as your Heavenly Father is perfect,' He was addressing all of us. For me the one condition most necessary is a state of grace, to be in the light of God, to do His will and to obey His commandments. To give oneself up to Him totally and dispose oneself as one would in a hairdresser's chair, with full confidence that the hairdresser knows his job and will do it well.

When I am communing with God in this ecstatic way, the use of my faculties and bodily senses is entirely in God's hands. It is a prayer which takes my whole person, and I allow the mover of these senses and faculties to be God. I am aware of what is happening to me, and I am sometimes even directing questions to God, but I leave the greatest active part to Him. As I enter into this prayer, there comes in me a power which puts me at ease and makes me relax, as if to say, 'Let the body function according to our directives.' With this relaxation the spiritual faculties take the upper hand in controlling the bodily senses. The body becomes weightless, the voice even in prayers said aloud cannot reach above a certain pitch — for instance when praying in tongues (i.e. in the language, sometimes incomprehensible to the speaker, which is uttered by those who are truly opened to the Holy Spirit). In this state it is impossible for anyone to be agitated or angry. Bodily reactions are fully controlled. God speaks in signs, pictures, whispers or inspirations. Every prayer that is said in this state is so meaningful and effective since there is no word which is superfluous.

There are some people who can be in this state for hours on end. But they should ask for the grace to co-operate with the Holy Spirit and to come back to earth without difficulty. There is no doubt at all that prayer is the best condition, but as long as we are still on earth we cannot lead two full lives. We should also avoid vanity, and telling of our experience at length when we are back to normal. Hence slowly we should acquire self-control even in this spiritual good.

What are the reasons which push a person into this kind of prayer? While stating them, one must avoid giving the impression that one is making rules for such prayer. Different people have their individual reasons, but having said this I can safely say that in my opinion the reasons may be two, just to shorten the story. One is that people experienced in prayer fail to get full satisfaction out of their prayer; they reach a stage where they just surrender themselves into the hands of God. One just says to oneself: 'I want to pray, and pray more. So I am going to rest in God's hands.' It is a spiritual rest in God's hands, or better still in God's bosom.

My second reason is that one is *pushed* to pray, if I can so express it, in the following aspects of prayer, and runs short of exact words to express what one wants to say to God:

1. Prayer of praise.
2. Prayer of thanksgiving.
3. Prayer of adoration.
4. Prayer of appeasement or atonement.
5. Prayer of petition.

Whether one wants to ask pardon for an offence against God or to thank God, in both cases it is impossible to pray in a way that will, on the one hand, adequately compensate for sin against God or, on the other, say 'thank you' to the full measure needed. The reason is that when God means to be kind to us, He is always taking His kindness to extremes. This means that we cannot use our own means, with full ownership of those means, to say 'thank you' to God. Both the means we use and we ourselves belong to God. So in the end what is 'thank you' to God? I can therefore say, even in regard to this second reason, that a person prays in this way having failed to reach personal satisfaction in saying a prayer of praise, thanksgiving, petition, pardon etc. According to this second reason, we go further than just totally resting in God; we say the prayers, sometimes even vocally, but they are a continuous repetition: 'Thank you Father. Thank you. Thank you Father. Thank you. I love you Father. I love you. I love you Father. How great you are. You are a great God. How great you are etc.' As we go on saying the same thing, slowly we enter a state of contemplation, and the soul is absorbed in prayer, while the bodily senses are neutralised. We are no longer aware of where we are. We do not feel the presence of those around us. We are completely captivated by the effects of our communion with the supernatural. There comes from above the true meaning of 'Thank you Father. I love you Father. How great you are.' The Supreme Father is felt to be at the end of the prayer, as an answer to the longing soul, which would like to say more but cannot. This meeting of the soul of the child and that of the Father results in the condition of ecstasy.

One wonders how a person can be absorbed in mere repetition of words. The fact is that although in prayer we repeat the same words, from the other side we receive varied inspirations. We may get a word of consolation from the Supreme Father: 'I am with you', 'Yes, I have received your thanks', 'Teach others to give praise to me.' God speaks to the person, while the person repeats the same words. Hence from time to time we may raise our voices higher and higher and even attempt to embrace God with our hands. Or we may just extend them upwards to the sky, or just open them as if we are receiving something from God. Our bodies have come to a standstill in the recitation of the prayer, and so we say the same thing. But our souls see and receive more than what is being repeated through our mouths.

What I have just described is a prayer which is willingly entered into by a longing soul. As I said, a soul which has failed to say more just surrenders itself by resting in God. Another soul may want to go on praying, but cannot find words to add new dimensions in its prayer. So it goes on praying by repeating the same words, not so much to add emphasis to the meaning, but rather aiming to reach a stage of satisfaction. In both cases the souls rest in God. They get their satisfaction from that fact, which can even be seen externally, that they are sensitive or conscious of where they are but their bodies can't respond to the situation. They are absorbed in the contemplation of God their Father. They are resting in Him.

When God speaks to us in the way of a spiritual conversation, it often happens that we react dramatically. We are as if taken aback. We seem not to be ready for the conversation. This is understood, because we have been made to converse with our fellow human beings, and not yet with the Supreme Father. We receive inspirations, revelations, directives, dreams, and so on, but not facing God. The presence of God in our souls is there as part of our being, since we are made in God's image. But we are too small to face God directly, and find ourselves completely inadequate to sustain His presence. Hence it is by His own power that God makes us able to take His messages, and transmit them as He wants them to be transmitted. That is how He managed to speak to the people I mentioned above, and how He sustained them Himself. His presence in them this time was not just His creative presence; on top of that He was speaking to them with His own personality. Most of them were shocked, or tried to refuse to carry out the message because they realised that they were so small before God or did not feel fit to be divine messengers.

. However, He has still been present in human society through touching many souls who have carried out His many missions to the different nations. He touches them in dreams, visions or apparitions, or merely through a voice in a room, in a church or a place convenient to Him. Most of these messengers go into ecstasy. I have never heard of a person who spoke to God here on earth with the full human senses. To meet the divine, one needs to be uplifted to the divine atmosphere, which is far superior to this earthly atmosphere; this parallels the superiority of the soul over the body. God uses the soul and its spiritual faculties to achieve His ends through our instrumentality. Some of these messengers are found in prayer. Others are carrying out their day-to-day duties, but all the time when they are in contact with God, they behave differently.

In both cases — when we are longing to express ourselves in depth through prayer, and God is in contact with us to communicate a special message — we in these two cases act above bodily consciousness, and for a while share supernaturality. We are made divine. We are spiritually conscious and alert, which is to say that the soul is in full contact with its Creator, God the Supreme Father. 'Everyone moved by the spirit is a son of God. The spirit you received is not the spirit of slaves bringing fear into your lives again; it is the spirit of sons, and it makes us cry out "*Abba*, Father". The spirit himself and our spirit bear united witness that we are children of God' (Romans 8. 14—17).

When all that is required to be a child of God has been gone into, we should do all we can to make this knowledge of prayer available to as many people as possible. That is why I congratulate the Yogi who have embraced the 'Karma Yoga' (Yoga of action); which means that in whatever activity one is engaged, one has to keep one's mind set in the remembrance of God. This remembrance is a continual check upon one's activity. To remember God also means to call upon God to be witness to one's action. And certainly with all the respect, reverence and love one has for God as Supreme Father, one cannot call Him witness to an evil action. I feel that this is one of our common missions to the many people in the world who live as if they are their own masters. God as their Supreme Father must be preached from the roof-tops, everywhere. This is the only way to save the world from the imminent danger of self-destruction through atheism and immorality in which it is.

(*Morality and Virtue*, pp. 7–28)

[Like so many of his generation outside Africa, Milingo has felt compelled to revise much of what he learnt when he was young. In a new booklet *My Prayers are not Heard* (1982) he writes:]

It took me forty-five years to brush away from my mind wrong concepts of God, wrong concepts of prayer, wrong concepts of Christianity. . . . I began to be trained as a churchman from the age of twelve, so I had all the opportunity to choose what was right and wrong. . . . My first wrong was my attitude to prayer. To me prayer was a religious imposition on those who accepted to become slaves of God. As they prayed, so I believed, they renewed to God their pledge of loyalty and subservience. . . . Today when I look back I can't believe what I was. In the history of the world we have come across cruel emperors, kings, queens and political leaders who imposed on their subjects certain slogans to be uttered at certain times. I believed that prayer too was an imposed slogan. . . .

However I changed when I read what Cardinal Newman wrote on the theme in his article 'Praying without ceasing': 'But as our bodily life discovers itself by its activity, so is the presence of the Holy Spirit in us discovered by a spiritual activity, and this activity is the spirit of continual prayer. Prayer is to the spiritual life what the beating of the pulse and the drawing of the breath are to the life of the body.' It took me forty-five years to have a glimpse of what prayer is. It is not a slogan. Don't ask me the

number of years of theological courses I followed without understanding the importance and necessity of prayer in my own personal life. I am ashamed to say it. . . . Cardinal Newman also
says: 'It would be as absurd to suppose that life could last when
the body was cold and motionless and senseless, as to call a soul
alive which does not pray. The state or habit of spiritual life
exerts itself, consists, in the continual activity of prayer'
(Newman, *Christian Readings*, vol. II).

(*My Prayers are not Heard*, pp. 9—10)

[The quotations from Newman show that while Milingo may reject
some of the attitudes he was taught, he is firmly centred in the great
traditions of the Church. He says himself:]

Vatican Council II has already done the job for us. Our own
Church realised that eras come and go. Values, even spiritual
values, are not applicable to all times. The Church of yesterday,
before Vatican II, was like the Old Testament is relation to the
New Testament. In the Old Testament there were a thousand
and one laws . . . the New Testament emphasised human dignity. 'The Sabbath was made for man and not man for the Sabbath' (Mark 2.27). In Vatican II the same thing has happened
. . . This emphasis on human dignity does not mean that we
now have no laws; we still have laws but they are not to be obeyed
as if they were the purpose of our being. They are to guide us in
our lives in order to attain the purpose for which we have become
Christians. The hinge on which all Church laws should hang is
love. Let us see how the AMECEA puts it in the booklet *The
Church and the Local Community*: 'The leader of this new people is Christ; its heritage is the dignity and freedom of the sons of
God; its law is the new commandment of love; its aim is the kingdom of God — already begun here on earth, but always growing until He brings it to perfection at the end of time.'

(Sermon at the Jubilee celebrations of the archdiocese of
Lusaka, 16 July 1978, pp. 10—11)

[The implementation of Vatican II and the missionary encyclicals is
not yet complete. They depend for their implementation on human
beings, and it is not surprising that many still cling to older ways. But
in his acceptance of the new vision, the supposed rebel Milingo
appears to come closer to the developing mind of the Church than
most of his critics.]

EPILOGUE

In April 1982 Archbishop Milingo was abruptly summoned to Rome following an investigation and report on his archdiocese called for by the Sacred Congregation for the Propagation of the Faith, the Vatican department concerned with missions, and conducted by two Kenyan prelates, Cardinal Maurice Ortunga and Bishop Nicodemo Kirima of Mombasa. After his arrival in Rome, he was forbidden to be in contact with his diocese, particularly the diocesan clergy and the Sisters of the congregation he founded — Daughters of the Redeemer. Thus he has never had the opportunity to say farewell to the diocese that he had ruled and to which he had given his whole life for fourteen years. This, to an African, is especially grievous.

For some time before that, he had felt he was under suspicion and being watched, but three particular events in the previous years led up to the climax. The first was the celebration of his fiftieth birthday on 15 June 1980, when he was asked to combine the celebrations with a Confirmation service at Kabwe (formerly Broken Hill), a town where he had strong support. Knowing his people, he suggested that they should sit down at the time of Confirmation to avoid any disorder, but in spite of this many were 'overcome', and there was confusion. All this was reported to the Papal pro-Nuncio Monsignor George Zur, who then wrote to all the Zambian bishops accusing Milingo of having broken his promise not to conduct healing in public (see *Demarcations*, pp. 46–7).

At the end of 1981 Milingo came home from abroad to find two more pitfalls awaiting him. The first did not appear very serious at the time but had repercussions later. It concerned a Mr Damian Mwale, who was in charge of the archdiocesan choir, which Milingo describes as a pilot choir chosen to experiment with liturgical improvements and adaptations (Milingo has himself written an African Mass which is regularly performed at the Cathedral). Mr Mwale was alleged to have 'slapped' a European nun — presumably in the heat of a choir practice in the local parish church. His choir had been chosen to sing at the forthcoming Peace Day Mass on 3 January 1982, in the presence of President Kaunda. Because the incident with the nun was still being investigated, the Vicar-General, Father Frank Taylor, is reported to have told Mr Mwale that he would not be allowed to conduct the choir on the great occasion, and that if he persisted in doing so he would 'be digging his own grave'. Mwale took the latter words literally, believed his life was threatened, and called in the police who went with him to the newly-returned Archbishop, to whom he looked as a protector and friend, asking him to settle the matter. The Vicar-General then told the Archbishop, who had supposed that tempers had cooled in his absence, that although no complaint had been received from the parish concerned, the whole matter was already in the hands of the pro-Nuncio. Milingo comments that this meant 'that the pro-Nuncio would already have made up his mind that if Archbishop Milingo will accept Mr Mwale as choirmaster in spite of the fact that he has slapped Sister X., it seems he is not doing his duty.' It would also mean 'that he is against missionaries and that they have no protection from him. This would add to the already filled cup of Milingo's faults which is waiting for just a few more incidents in order for him to be condemned' (Archdiocesan Report by Milingo). These comments reflect the state of mutual mistrust which had arisen between the Archbishop and the pro-Nuncio. The Archbishop was able to persuade the choirmaster to step down, but that was not the end of the affair. Later in 1982, when Milingo was already in Rome, Damian Mwale was one of those who circulated and got printed in the Zambian press papers which the Church authorities allege to be forgeries: a report under the names of Father Frank Taylor and Father Andreas Edele (a German), the Archbishop's Pastoral Secretary, to the pro-Nuncio criticising Milingo and the African clergy in racialist terms; and subsequently a letter purportedly from Father Stanislaus Walscak, the Procurator of the archdiocese, asking for protection for white priests on account of public reaction to this forged report. There was internal evidence that these papers were forged, and cases for forgery and libel have been brought in the Zambian Courts. The case is *sub judice* at the time of going to press.

The case of Damian Mwale was with the pro-Nuncio concurrently with another more distressing and disturbing case concerning one of the Sisters of 'the Pious Union of the Daughters of the Redeemer', the community of nuns referred to above, in whose house Milingo had taken refuge when driven from his official residence. The Sister had been away on a course in Kenya and on her return her companions noticed that she had got fat (she had probably been better fed, the Zambian nuns being very poor and their diet sparse). It was suggested that she was pregnant, and public gossip implicated Milingo. He was informed of this, and with difficulty the nun was persuaded by him to submit to a medical examination so as to silence rumour. This was carried out by the Polish woman doctor who, with her husband, gave her services free to the archdiocese. She found that the Sister was not pregnant, but suspected fibroids and referred her to the gynaecology department of the University Teaching Hospital (UTH). Milingo was then abroad for a month, and on his return, finding that the examination had not been made, he wrote to the consultant concerned asking that it might take place quickly 'so that if she needs an operation we may submit her quickly to the appropriate doctors' (Archdiocesan Report). He gave this letter to his secretary to type, and she, jumping to the conclusion that an abortion was being asked for, showed it to Father Edele, the Pastoral Secretary. Father Edele took the letter straight to the pro-Nuncio without seeking the permission of the Archbishop, saying that he could not bear such hypocrisy, since Milingo had publicly opposed abortion. Although by that time a report from UTH had said that no operation was needed, the pro-Nuncio ordered a further examination by a doctor of his choice. The poor Sister, who by then had already been examined three times, refused, and only Milingo was able to persuade her, after much prayer, to be examined once more, by a religious doctor, Sister Mary Monica Tyndall of UTH. Her report confirmed that the Sister was not and had never been pregnant, and Sister Tyndall accompanied the pro-Nuncio who went in person to the Convent to read out the report and apologise to the Sisters (Archdiocesan Report).

The distress caused to a very religious woman, the ungrounded suspicion held against her and the unsympathetic way she had been treated greatly upset Milingo, who had suffered with her and upheld her in her ordeal. His own views on priestly celibacy and sexual morality are very firm, and are matters of heartfelt personal conviction, as can be seen in his addresses to priests. He had always been aware that his enemies would like to trap him with a woman, and said so in his earliest book, *Healing* (p.21). He talks there of the problem of his many women patients:

When the Lord spoke to me He did not tell me to use different methods, one for men and another for women. To my reaction in 1974 when I saw so many women coming to me, He answered me with his Mother Mary; 'We shall let you know those who have evil intentions, and we shall protect you.' They have kept their promise, and I sincerely thank them for being so close to me in these difficult moments, when I deal with hundreds of women in a month. I have come across very few women, I can count them on my fingers, who had misguided intentions. But it is hard for them to do anything with me when the powers of the Lord are in me; and from me to them it is impossible. This applies to both men and women. So I may assure my friends and my accusers that the divine origin of the powers is not proved or disproved in treating women, by the awareness — or lack of awareness — of them as sex objects; but rather by respecting them as persons who have a right to be whole, and therefore have a right to these powers for any purpose for which they feel and believe they should be used. On my part any disease a woman tells me of must be treated as I am directed, and I should not in any way diminish the measure of the cure by asking God that since I am a man He should change me into a woman in order to treat a woman.

(*Healing*, pp. 22–3)

The Archbishop's state of mind after these events could not have made it easy for him to be tolerant with those who had been involved. The episode ended his close friendship with Father Edele, his Pastoral Secretary, who had been at his side in the work of the Zambian Helpers' Society, which Milingo had founded in 1966 to provide mobile clinics. Father Edele, who had reported the matter to the pro-Nuncio, sent in his resignation on 19 December 1981, the day Sister Tyndall's report was taken to the Convent. A few days later the Vicar-General, Father Frank Taylor, also resigned, apparently after a stormy interview with the Archbishop. The resignation of these two priests gave rise to rumours and suggestions of misconduct on Milingo's part, originating in Zambia early in 1983 and reaching Europe later that year. It seems clear that these priests, and probably others, had been dealing with the pro-Nuncio, over Milingo's head, in matters where the judgement should have been Milingo's. He had been treated without due respect, or even human charity, and in fact ostracised. I believe that the Cardinal Prefect of the Office for the Propagation of the Faith (Propaganda Fide) was himself in Lusaka in January 1982, and it would have been he who initiated the investigation by Cardinal Ortunga and Bishop Kirima, and who would have had a part in the Papal summons. Cardinal Ortunga's report was never made public, nor was it ever shown to Milingo so that he could have replied to its findings.

Archbishop Milingo was called to Rome in April 1982. For a while after his arrival he was kept incommunicado, and charged not to appear in public places in case he should be questioned, or to attend Charismatic services with the groups he was familiar with. This treatment alarmed his Italian friends and they began to agitate for his case to be heard. News of it got back to Zambia where there were angry protests, and a Christian Action Group was formed to demand his return. This was headed by an Anglican, Simon Mwamba, Director of the Government's Mechanical Services Department. There were also Anglican protests in the newspapers. The Action Group even threatened to set up a breakaway church, but this Milingo would never have encouraged. He had said that it never entered his mind to do anything which would drive him out of the Church which he loves (Milingo's notes). He has faithfully obeyed its commands, although he has been sorely tried.

After his arrival in Rome, Milingo was given medical and psychiatric tests, but for the latter the psychiatrist found it unnecessary to continue after the first interview. He was examined four times on doctrine in formal question-and-answer sessions by the Cardinal Prefect of the Propaganda Fide — whose responsibility is for the Church in 'missionary countries'. (In a sense the hierarchies of those countries, such as Zambia, are not independent, hence the large part played by the Papal representative in the affairs of the archdiocese of Lusaka.) With the Cardinal Prefect was the Secretary General of the Congregation for the Evangelisation of Peoples, and two others. Archbishop Milingo complains that at these sessions he was alone, one against four, and that he was not allowed to have with him a witness or counsellor, although this was normal practice. In the interrogation he was accused of introducing words of his own, some of them 'in tongues', into the rite of Confirmation. He answered that this was a common practice among the Charismatics, and that a white priest in Zambia, Father Faulhaber, had done the same without being censured. He explained his reasons more fully: 'I base my additional prayer on this text in Holy Scripture, Romans 8. 26−7: "The Spirit too comes to help us in our weakness. For when we cannot choose words in order to pray properly, the Spirit himself expresses our plea in a way we could never have put into words." I add this prayer in order to be with it and in it: "Lord, if I should be the cause of failure of the coming of the Holy Spirit, overlook what I am and send your Spirit all the same." That is the intention, but the actual prayer is not known to me since I say it in tongues' (Milingo's notes). Another point raised by the Cardinal Prefect was that in Lusaka lay people had been allowed to anoint the sick. Milingo replied that this was also a practice in the Charismatic movement, and was not intended to replace the sacrament of Extreme Unction (ibid.). (Priests are scarce in Africa, and healing by lay groups is encouraged in some places. The group in Lusaka prays in unison, the people extending their arms towards any in the congregation who need healing.) Milingo believes that the result of the interrogation was a foregone conclusion, that Rome was only playing for time, and that it was decided from the first that he should not return to Lusaka. He mentions that in all the questioning he was never asked about any positive developments in his archdiocese, although he had been there for fourteen years and had achieved a great deal.

However, in a final attempt to discredit him there were accusations of mismanagement of the archdiocesan finances. These came from the caretaker Archbishop, Elias Mutale, who had found a larger deficit than he expected. Archbishop Milingo had been bundled out of Zambia at a moment's notice, without any chance to hand over to

Mutale, or to pay his own debts if he had any. He says that he handed over to the Administrator and Treasurer of the archdiocese, Father Walsack, 30,000 kwacha (approximately £7,000 or $10,000) in cash, and received for his journey 1,000 Deutchmarks. There was about £10,000 in credits to come in to the archdiocese, which had a credit balance of K71,479.76 and liabilities of K72,800.00, which would thus seem to have been almost entirely covered (Milingo's notes). There were also several accounts in banks abroad. Milingo says that he never had a personal foreign bank account. One of the accounts, at the Hypo Bank, Munich, which he has been accused of keeping secret, was in the name of the Daughters of the Redeemer, and is used for the maintenance of Sisters studying abroad. Withdrawals from it required the signatures of two of the Sisters as well as that of the Archbishop. The main account of the archdiocese was also at Munich with the Deutsche Bank. Accusations that Milingo had misused CAFOD funds, paid into one of these accounts, was firmly denied by the Director of CAFOD, Julian Filochowski, in a letter published in *The Tablet* of 22 October 1983. (Father Walscak told me in answer to a direct question that the Archbishop had left the financial management entirely to him.) The Archbishop never had a regular salary or allowance, but depended on donations from the parishes he visited. The problem of foreign exchange is always acute in Zambia; donations in foreign currencies are better kept abroad because there are no goods or services to be bought with them in the country, but on the other hand Zambian kwacha may not be taken out. During his archepiscopate Milingo built the Cathedral in Lusaka, and one other church; the building fund with the National Westminster Bank in England is, not surprisingly, exhausted, but there seems to be no debt on the buildings, surely something exceptional.

During the first eighteen months of his forcible stay in Rome, Milingo was not allowed an audience with the Pope. He was being pressed to resign, and given the alternative of being either a healer or an archbishop. There were no further objections to his healing. He was in great distress over the decision he had to take, and he eventually went into a three-day retreat to pray over it. He decided he would not resign until he had spoken to the Pope, and although he had tried many times unsuccessfully to gain an audience, he now wrote a detailed letter which reached the Holy Father. As a result his case was taken over from the Office of the Propaganda Fide to the Pope's own Secretariat in the Vatican. He says, 'From the day my case was in the hands of the Holy Father I once more became a free citizen in the Church' (private letter). The Pope told him that the bishops in Zambia would not allow him back, because they said he could not manage the archdiocese but that his vocation was for healing. The Pope, in the private audience he gave to Milingo on 6 July 1983, told him, 'We shall safeguard your healing apostolate' (quoted in a private letter from Milingo).

He gave his motive for agreeing to resign as a desire to avoid causing disunity in his former archdiocese. Given the state of misunderstanding and suspicion, it seems doubtful if he could have returned with any hope of finding peace when he arrived. It remains that there has been a species of trial without any charges, and an acquittal which has never been promulgated. As he says, '*Roma locuta*' has not meant '*causa finita*'. He has obeyed but his detractors have not, and continue to attack his character without his being able to reply. When recently he made a healing mission to Nairobi, Kenya, Cardinal Ortunga would not allow him to use any church for healing, or to preach at the University Chaplaincy. He is free to travel, as on this Kenya mission, and he holds healing services in Rome. Since he left Zambia he has travelled to a number of parts of the world including Australia, the United States and the West Indies. He has been given an appointment as Special Delegate to the Pontifical Commission for Migration and Tourism. As such he is in charge of the spiritual care of migrants, refugees and Christian tourists and is directly responsible to the Holy Father. Yet, in default of any statement from those whose accusations removed him from his see, it can only be supposed that his fault lay in his outspoken criticism of the Missions, and that his popularity with his own people threatened the Church's comfortable *status quo*.

BIBLIOGRAPHICAL NOTE

The following Vatican documents on Mission are relevant for the consideration of the life and writings of Archbishop Milingo:

Papal Encyclicals and Apostolic Letters on Mission

30 Nov. 1919. Apostolic Letter *Maximum Illud* of Benedict XV.*
28 Feb. 1926. Encyclical Letter *Rerum Ecclesiae* of Pius XI.*
2 June 1951. Encyclical Letter *Evangelii Praecones* of Pius XII.*
21 April 1957. Encyclical Letter *Fidei Donus* of Pius XII.*
26 Nov. 1959. Encyclical Letter *Princeps Pastorum* of John XXIII.*
8 Dec. 1975. Apostolic Exhortation *Evangelii Nuntiandi* of Paul VI.*

Documents relating to the Second Vatican Council

7 Dec. 1963. Decree *Ad Gentes* on the Church's missionary activity.†
6 Aug. 1966. Norm for implementation *Ecclesiae Sanctae* of Paul VI.‡

Papal Messages and Addresses on Mission

29 Oct. 1967. Message *Africae Terrarum* of Paul VI.*
31 Jan. 1969. Kampala Address of Paul VI.*
3 May 1980. Address to the Bishops of Zaire by John Paul II.*

Synod of Bishops in Rome on Mission

1974. Bishops of Africa, Report on the Church in Africa.*
1977. Address to the Bishops of Africa by Paul VI.*

Sources for the above:
*Raymond Hickey, OSA (*ed.*), *Modern Missionary Documents and Africa* (Dominican Publications, Dublin, 1982).
†Austin Flannery, OP (*ed.*), *Vatican Council II: the Conciliar and Post-Conciliar Documents* (Fowler Wright, 1981).
‡Catholic Truth Society, S. 312.